This
Is
Not
About
You

A Menmoir

This Is Not About You

Rosemary Mac Cabe

unbound

First published in 2023

Unbound
c/o TC Group, 6th Floor King's House, 9-10 Haymarket,
London SW1Y 4BP
www.unbound.com

© Rosemary Mac Cabe, 2023

This book is a work of non-fiction based on the life, experiences and
recollections of the author. In some cases names of people, places, dates,
sequences or the detail of events have been changed to protect the
privacy of others. The author has stated to the publishers that, except in
such respects not affecting the substantial accuracy of the work, the
contents of this book are true.

Typeset by Jouve (UK), Milton Keynes

A CIP record for this book is available from the British Library

ISBN 978-1-80018-243-1 (paperback)
ISBN 978-1-80018-245-5 (ebook)

Printed in Great Britain by Clays Ltd, Elcograf S.p.A.

3 5 7 9 8 6 4 2

To my mum, who will hate this

To my aunt, who will have her own...

'We are given a single story line about what makes a good life, even though not a few who follow that story line have bad lives. We speak as though there is one good plot with one happy outcome, while the myriad forms a life can take flower – and wither – all around us.'

Rebecca Solnit, 'The Mother of All Questions', *Harper's Magazine*

Contents

Preface

This may, at first glance, look like a book about dating. It may look like a book about a handful of specific men, and the impact they had on my life. It may look like a tell-all, a salacious insight into my sex life, something about which you may or may not be curious.

It may well look like a lot of things, but this book is really about discovery. It is about searching for meaning in a series of romantic relationships. It is about the chokehold I have allowed my core socialisation as a woman, at least when it comes to the importance of having a significant relationship with a man, to have over my entire life.

It is about me – how I've changed and how I've stayed the same; how much bad behaviour I have accepted because I wanted men to love me, and how much bad behaviour I have indulged in because I wanted men to love me.

It is about the idea of romance and the concept of love and the reality of both (and neither). For once, though, it is not about the men in question. For once, these men are the objects; I am the subject. Me, me, me.

If there is a lesson to be learned from all of this, I think it is: focus more on yourself. Ask what it is that *you* want. Ask who it is that *you* would be, if you were given the freedom to decide. Then give yourself that freedom, because no one else is going to give it to you.

(Almost) all names have been changed.

The Beginnings

I have been in a relationship for the better part of my thirty-eight years. That's an odd sentence to write down – I haven't been in any one relationship for longer than five. Rather, I have been in and out of a variety of relationships with a variety of men for more than two decades. Yes, it is men I am attracted to – a fact that causes me no small degree of shame, frustration and regret. Not to say that I'm attracted to men in general, but, rather, to specific men. Some men. (Not all men – but, I will admit, too many men.)

My first relationship started when I was three. It was not, I can see now, consensual. My cousin Alex is a year older than I am and did not in any way return my affections, which manifested as my wanting to hold his hand at each and every given opportunity.

He reminded me of Peter from the BBC adaptation of *The Lion, the Witch and the Wardrobe*, one of six forms of entertainment we owned on Betamax and, as a consequence, a series I watched on repeat. Alex had – has – rosebud lips and rosy cheeks and perfectly straight, chestnut-brown hair. There is a photograph of us, taken in 1988: a close-up portrait. I have pressed my face against his and am squinting into the sunlight, smiling for the camera (and, I suspect, for him). It is the happiest I have ever looked in a photograph.

I have been known to make a lot of life decisions for – and because of – the man I am dating at that moment. Some have been of little consequence: 'Henry doesn't like that cinema, so we always go to the one that's forty-five minutes away.' Others have been more significant: 'I don't think I'll take my Erasmus year in Italy; I took that year off before university and now I'm already behind my friends.' Translation: I have a boyfriend. Please, don't make me leave him behind.

I have spent a lot of my time feeling regretful about the power I have given these relationships. I should be okay being alone. I shouldn't need, of all the things a woman could need, a man.

In my twenties, my sister – older than I am by six years and wiser than I am by an infinite, unknowable amount – urged me to spend some time being single. I understood this to mean that she thought I should spend time fucking around, kissing strange men in nightclubs and letting them touch me in dark corners or, should circumstances allow, back in their bedrooms. It was only later that I realised what she truly had in mind: that I dedicate at least a small portion of my life to discovering what it is that *I* like, what it is that *I* want to do, alone, away from the influence of whatever man I am currently trying to please.

It felt as though the very notion of 'being single',

the idea that there were all of these adventures to be had while single, was a far-off one. That was something to think about at some unknown date, in an unknown future. Why, in the here and now, would I turn away from a potential romance for the sake of experiencing a singlehood I might not even enjoy? (Chances of enjoyment seemed slim; I'd seen *Bridget Jones's Diary* and *She's All That* and *Bring It On*, and if there was one thing I knew for certain, it was that women were infinitely happier in a couple than they were out of one.)

By the time I began – slowly, grudgingly, reluctantly – to accede to her directive, it was, at least biologically speaking, too late. I had, almost inadvertently, had my fertility tested: while working as a journalist and occasional television panel guest, I was asked to take part in a segment on twentysomethings and fertility. The plan was to go for a simple blood test, which would reveal my egg count, and then appear on an afternoon magazine show, alongside a fertility doctor, to discuss the results.

As it happened, my results weren't good. 'You have the egg count we'd expect to see in a woman of forty-four,' a nurse told me, not unkindly (although, a bit unkindly, in hindsight?) over the phone. I was twenty-five. And, though I had no plans to get pregnant – in fact, I had been convinced, for most of my life, that I was not the mothering kind – I was shocked at the idea that I no longer had the choice. I cried (very professionally, dabbing at my eyes with a fabric handkerchief) at my desk and subsequently decided not to appear on television to discuss my uterine failure.

All of a sudden, it felt as though everything I had known to be true had been turned upside down. I really *didn't* have all the time in the world to spend being single; I no longer had my whole life ahead of me. Time, like life, is finite, at least for me, my eggs, my biological destiny. I couldn't really afford to fuck around any more, either literally or figuratively.

My therapist would later touch on my serial monogamy, my intense desire to be in a relationship at all times, I think, by accident. We were talking about something else – my then-upcoming visit to the US, a three-month trip that I was considering extending, depending on the outcome of a visa application I would make later that year. I was cautiously optimistic. I talked about my worry that I wouldn't make any friends, that I would end up alone, far away from the people I love.

'I'm not worried about that,' she told me. 'You're someone who thrives on relationships – you will undoubtedly find someone to spend your time with. It's something that's important to you.' She said it without judgement, and it was an observation I received without shame. Some people love shopping. Other people love being in relationships. (There are worse things I could do.)

I had always been told that the only way one could actually, properly, thoroughly find oneself was through the act of being alone. Only that alone-ness itself would allow a person to shine a light on why they opted to sit in the cinema aisle, why the window seat on a plane was always the preference. Without someone else to appease, you'd know what it is you really wanted to do on a Sunday morning. Do I really like lie-ins? Do I really love Sunday brunch? Do I feel like something sweet, or something savoury?

But I somehow managed to find myself – to learn who it is that I am, and what it is that I like – via a series of serious and semi-serious (though never casual) relationships. I have cemented the foundation of my personality with the help of a series of romantic supports. I have allowed my love life to act as a sort of scaffolding to the building blocks of my own personal development and, honestly? I don't feel as if I know myself any less than I would had I spent five years truly concentrating on being single.

Of course, there is no way of knowing. I cannot go back. I wouldn't want to. There are certain moments, sure, that I would return to – the way I used to rewind a tape, to listen to my favourite song, over and over again; the way my nephew rewinds to the very start of *Rescue Bots*, four times minimum, so that he can listen to the theme tune. It's his favourite part of the whole show. But a total do-over? No, thanks. I'll stick with what I did, when I did it, and why. After all, if I hadn't, I wouldn't be where I am now.

My last major breakup happened after five years together, for reasons I can't quite grasp, even now. I know that we had been happy, because I wrote it down. I told people. They tell me now, they reassure me: 'He did love you – of course he did! And you loved him.' But I can't access the emotion any more. It's weird how that happens. I can see the memories, playing out on screen, inside my head. I can remember thinking about how much I loved him. But I can't remember the feeling, not really.

When I think of him now, it is as if we were actors. We met during rehearsals for a play about two people who meet and fall for one another, a play that turned out to be about the slow, achingly painful death of love. When we see each other now, I feel vaguely embarrassed. Here is a man with whom I shared several sex scenes. Here is a man who saw me in the bath, who changed the bedsheets after, in the throes of a vomiting bug, a particularly violent retch caused me to wet myself, soaking both the sheets and my pyjamas in the process.

Here is a man who sat in front of me, and I in front of him, and discussed marriage and children and a future that seemed so neatly laid out. Here is a man for whom I played a part. Here is a man for whom I became motherly and nurturing, but also tempestuous and insecure. Here is a man for whom I changed.

In a way, I changed for all of them. I look back on each version of myself – on the roles I played, roles that depended entirely on the character I was cast against – and I feel the heat rising in my cheeks. I am not someone who embarrasses easily, but my willingness to cast off so much of myself feels shameful to me now.

Change is, of course, inevitable. We teach one

another things; we open doors that had previously looked like lines in the wall, cracks in the plasterwork. We serve as a sort of guide for the people in our lives, as they do for us. I know this. Not all change is bad.

I will never know what I would have been like if I had never met these men. I'm sure there would have been other men and other ideals to measure myself against. Instead of becoming a *Star Wars* fan, I might have feigned an interest in American football, eventually learning the rules, growing invested in the teams, appreciating the skill and adrenaline and excitement of a high-stakes game. I'm glad *Star Wars* won out.

It doesn't matter to me, not any more, what these men think of me. They don't need to know what a good actor I am. It will make no difference to their lives.

But it did make a difference to mine. In a way, going through these relationships has been a retracing of steps, a redrawing of the map. I can see what brought me here, there, to this conclusion.

As I write this, my baby is bouncing in his Jumperoo behind me. It is jungle-themed, so it plays music punctuated by elephant noises. He has just learned to spit, so he blows loud raspberries at entirely irregular intervals. Each one surprises me.

My American husband is at work. He didn't kiss me goodbye this morning; he leaves before I have awoken, before I want to acknowledge that one day is done and another has begun.

He will be home later with my stepsons – boys of ten and eight, from his previous marriage. Before moving to the US, I would honestly never have considered dating someone who was divorced. I balked at the notion of being with someone who had children – I was sure they would take priority over us and our relationship. But once I joined American Tinder, I noticed that everyone in my age bracket was divorced, with one, if not two or three, children, some of whom were already in their teens.

They marry early in the Midwest, and unlike in Ireland, they do not blink at the idea of marrying twice, even three times.

One of the first men I got talking to asked me – and I will admit I was offended, although I don't believe he meant it to come across as anything more than simple curiosity – why it was that I had never married, as if I were the spinster aunt in a Brontë novel. Like I said: American.

Everything I've done has brought me here. The men I surrounded myself with led to my being, ultimately, surrounded by men. The irony is not lost on me.

I am grateful for it all, but only because of its conclusion. There are moments I am ashamed of and decisions that I regret and men I wish to apologise to, and yes, men I wish would, even now, apologise to me.

This book is not about them, though, not really. It's about me: how I made and unmade myself for each of them. It's about memory and perception and reality and how I chose to present myself, on a platter, to so many men, many of whom would prove themselves entirely unworthy of me.

There is nothing in the pages of this book that is untrue, even if the men in question may remember it differently. If, that is, they remember it at all. I have learned that moments of significance are not always significant to everyone involved.

Henry

In another life – maybe in another book – Henry would hold a certain significance, as the man to whom I 'lost' my virginity. *My first love*, I would think, wistfully, remembering this tall, older man – he was eighteen, while I was sixteen, a mere child – and I would reminisce about the wonderful times we shared, the love that blossomed that summer.

As it happens, ours was not a love story for the ages. His is not a face I think about all that often. I mean, fine, every few months I see something that reminds me of him: an Aaliyah album cover; a bare midriff; a tall man with an aquiline nose and the kind of glint in his eye that *should* make you think he's up to no good, but instead makes you wonder if he'd be interested in getting up to no good with you.

I stumbled across Henry's wedding photos on social media recently. When you are Irish, you stumble across a lot of things about your exes, whether you're looking for them or not. Everyone knows someone who knows someone *you* know. There are never more than three degrees of separation – if even that – between one Irish person and another.

In the name of full disclosure, though, I would like to clarify: I can't say for certain that I *wasn't* looking for them.

Henry is now married to a friend of a friend. Like I said: three degrees of separation. They show up on each other's social media pages sometimes. I wonder, a lot, what my friend thinks of him – in photos, he gives the impression of being the doting dad, the loving husband. I can't quite align this image of him as a man with the memory I have of him as a boy.

It is entirely possible, I know, that this is who he is now; after all, when I knew him, he was a teenager, newly emerged from childhood. He will forever be that young fella to me – funny, a little full of himself, a glint in his eye and entirely untrustworthy. Although I wouldn't find that out until the end.

When we met, he was dating my friend Laura. I'm not sure, at the time, we would have called it 'dating', but they were meeting up in the local shopping centre, holding hands in a booth in Pizza Hut, disappearing around the corner before we went to catch our bus home so that they could kiss – with tongues! – in privacy.

I remember chatting with her, on the bus on the way home, about how much she liked him; about what a great kisser he was; about whether or not he would ask her to be his girlfriend. She was especially enamoured with how tall he was; she was among the tallest girls in our year, and Henry was one of the first boys she'd ever been truly interested in, in part because she didn't tower over him, something that was then – and is now – important to her.

To the casual observer, I think it probably looked like I just wanted to prove that I could take something that belonged to someone else. But that's not quite right. I didn't want to take this boy from her, necessarily; I wanted him to choose me, to decide that I was, after all, the one he wanted.

In school, I never felt like anyone's first choice. In physical education, when we would line up and divide into teams, I was never among the first (or even second, or third). I wouldn't always be last, but I was close enough for it to sting. In hindsight, given my abject terror of any spherical object approaching me at speed, it makes sense.

But it was the same routine with things I was good at – spelling, memorising lines, remembering song lyrics, singing them out loud in front of an audience. One particular teacher would command us to 'raise your hand if you know the French for "audience"', and when my hand shot straight up into the air, he would glance at me dismissively and say, 'You can put your hand down – I know *you* know.'

When Henry first texted me, Laura was on holiday in Europe with her parents and, honestly, it seemed innocent. Of course, I know that game now. I know what it feels like when men are testing the water, trying to see how far you'll go, how many items of clothing you'll take off for them.

His texts got flirtier and flirtier and I lapped them up. I was flattered. It made me feel good to think that, all these times we'd been hanging out as a group, trying to facilitate this romance between him and Laura, he'd been thinking about me. I tried to ignore the question of how it might have made *her* feel.

I called Laura, on her holidays, to confess my sins. It felt like it was the right thing to do. I remember her dad answering his mobile phone from Spain, probably assuming someone had died – in 2001, we didn't just *casually* call each other on anything bar the inexpensive landline – and putting me on to her. I think we both cried.

She was, understandably, shocked, angry, upset, disappointed – with me, more than with him, I'm sure. I grovelled an apology – I'm sure I told her that I hadn't meant it to happen, that *it just did*, that I couldn't help how I felt (and neither could he). I can't imagine these platitudes were in any way comforting.

By the time they got back, Henry was my boyfriend. Those kisses, snatched around the corner from the bus stop, the hand-holding in the booth of a cut-price restaurant, were all mine now.

Laura's parents didn't speak to me for at least a year after that fateful phone call, long after Henry was out of the picture, long after Laura had forgiven me. The roaming charges must have been salt in their wounds, but that didn't occur to me at the time. Though we didn't meet on a beach somewhere, ours truly was a summer romance – over before school began again in September. It felt like it lasted a lot longer at the time, but now, it feels like it all happened in the blink of an eye.

That summer, I got a job in a clothes shop in the city centre. It paid minimum wage, but in cash (no pesky taxes to worry about) and we got a generous 40 per cent discount on the merchandise.

On Saturdays, we would be dressed by the manager, who would select items for us from the new arrivals, or whatever was selling badly and they wanted to advertise. When the shop closed that evening, we would run around the corner to the dry cleaners with our day's outfit and check it in to be cleaned, so that it would be ready to be put back on the racks on Monday morning.

I remember, one particular Saturday, Henry came to meet me after work. He waited for me outside, leaning against one of the columns that divided the food court from the cheap accessories shop next door. 'Your boyfriend's waiting for you!' one of my fellow shop girls informed me with a smirk. I tried to feign embarrassment, but doubt anything could have masked the delighted look on my face.

When we'd finished folding and hanging and counting and dusting, I went outside to greet him, wearing the low-slung jeans and a tight red printed T-shirt I'd just bought with my weekly wages (at least three-quarters of which went straight back into that shop, frittered away on midriff-baring tees and overpriced denims).

'I like this look,' he said, gesturing to the two

inches of exposed skin between my waistband and the hem of my top. I don't think I had ever, before that, felt like someone thought I was sexy. The feeling was intoxicating.

We spent a lot of our time, that summer, with his friends. I would get dropped off at his house and we would take the bus, sitting upstairs, something I never did on my own. I was always afraid that I would find myself sitting too close to a group of intimidating teenagers; now, I was in the group.

After we got together, made it official, we stopped going to the nearby shopping centre, which had a cinema and a variety of fast food outlets and a games arcade. Henry said he hated it there, alluding to some kind of unjustified run-in with their security staff that had entirely put him off darkening the doorway.

Instead, we would take the bus all the way into the city centre, an hour each way, and then walk, in the rain, to the cinema, a fast food outlet, a different games arcade.

Much later, I would learn that there was no unjustified security-related incident, and that Henry did, in fact, frequently darken the doorway of that very same shopping centre. It was where his *other* girlfriend worked, stocking shelves and serving customers in the flagship supermarket on the lower-ground floor, and he couldn't risk us running into one another beneath the same roof. (Don't they say that how you get them is how you'll lose them? I hadn't heard that, back then, but I have now. It's one of those things they say.)

At some point along the way, I lost my virginity in the spare bedroom of his mum's semi-D.

As usual, we'd been hanging out in a group – me, Henry, a handful of his friends – playing computer games in his bedroom. This sounds like a cliché, but it was true: the walls were painted black and adorned with the type of posters adults thought of as heavy metal back then, but are probably closer to mainstream rock, in actuality – Limp Bizkit and Linkin Park and the odd Marilyn Manson.

I remember feeling aggrieved by how little attention I was being paid. Not yet driving, I had been dropped off by my parents, with the promise – or the threat – that they would be picking me up at 9 p.m., 'no later'. Our time was precious.

Henry's eyes were glued to the screen, his laughs reserved for his friends' jokes. We passed around a litre of Malibu rum, sipping warm coconut-flavoured alcohol straight from the bottle. I took small sips, trying to laugh at the right moments and look suitably invested in whatever game it was we were playing.

I remember leaning over to kiss him, pressing my body against his. I asked if he wanted to go downstairs, with a pointed look – I wanted him to stop spending time with them, these boys who were disturbing our alone time, and to focus his energy on me. We left the room together, hand in hand.

I wonder what they thought, as we walked out of the bedroom and down the stairs, into the spare room that had once been a garage. It was filled with suitcases and black plastic bags and a faded clothes horse whose metal had begun to rust at the corners, one side sagging under the weight of a duvet, clean but musty from the damp cold of that unheated room.

We took our own clothes off. As an adult, I like when someone takes my clothes off for me. I like to feel that they're invested in the experience. They can't wait for me to unbutton my blouse so they pull it off over my head. They unzip my jeans and slide a hand down the front of my knickers. They are overcome with want and it is passionate and messy and clumsy, and it is important to me that the desire is there.

Back then, in that unused downstairs bedroom, we undressed clinically and I lay down on the bed, legs spread. Henry rolled on a condom. I had heard horror stories about teenage pregnancies, girls whose futures were erased by the arrival of a screaming baby (and then, inevitably, a second), careers cut short by the shackles of parenthood.

I remember it being uncomfortable, but not painful – despite the fact that every teen girls' magazine I had ever read had warned me to expect searing pain, vast discomfort, blood everywhere, like a TV crime scene. It felt good, to have finally lost my virginity. At last, here was something significant I could cross off my to-do list.

It was a little like the time I'd had a verruca frozen off in the doctor's surgery: uncomfortable, but I had entered into this willingly. I was pretty sure I knew what to expect.

I lay down and I thought about how much better it would get and how we were, of course, now a *proper* couple. This is how we fall in love: on our backs, enduring a discomfort we willingly signed up for, hoping things will get better.

I was reminded, too, of the day I got my first period, on holiday in a friend's mobile home in Wexford, emerging from the bathroom, grinning widely.

'I need to talk to you about something,' I told my friend's mother, matter-of-factly.

Later, my friend told me I had not been subtle. 'It was *so* obvious,' she'd said, rolling her eyes.

It was okay for her – she'd got her period months before, maybe even a full year. I'd been left behind. I was a girl whose friends had become women overnight and were suddenly allowed to order from the main menu, while I was stuck with chicken goujons, chips and fizzy drinks.

I was neither the last of my friends to have sex nor the first, but it was important to me to experience this rite of passage. At sixteen, I was reading women's magazines and watching *Sex and the City* and I knew that sexuality was an important part of adult life. I don't think I was expecting any sensation to arise from the experience bar relief, maybe a little task-related satisfaction.

Afterwards, Henry asked if I was okay. I said yes, I was fine, that was nice. (It was not, but it was important to me, even then, not to hurt a man's feelings.) He kissed me on the lips and left me in the room, in the semi-darkness, to get myself together. I wondered if I should look around for the parts of me that had fallen off, to reassemble myself like a jigsaw. But whatever I'd lost was gone for good.

It's been a lifetime since I gave myself to my older boyfriend – at sixteen, eighteen seemed so incredibly adult – in his mother's spare room, lying on a white towel and thinking about our future. I can't remember if we ever had sex again – I can't remember if it did ever get better.

Things I can remember: when the R&B singer Aaliyah died in a plane crash, Henry called me, in tears, to talk about what a freak accident it was. I remember going to a family wedding with him, where one of his friends told me I was 'too good' for him.

I remember heading off on a three-week trip to the south of France, where I was doing an exchange with a French girl my mum had been put in touch with through the family she had worked for as an au pair in the 1960s. I cried as I went through security and the whole way to my gate, perhaps wondering if my going on holiday would encourage Henry to reach out to the next girl on his list.

I remember calling him from my host family's landline, and him telling me that he didn't want to be with me any more. I choked down sobs during dinner on the outside terrace. My temporary French dad disappeared halfway through, re-emerging clad only in a white sheet, a golden crown of thorns upon his head, reciting Shakespeare and assuring me that love is not love which alters when it alteration finds. I remember laughing through my tears.

Weeks later, a friend of my sister's – who worked in the same supermarket – would tell me that Henry was seeing one of her colleagues. In fact, she told me, he'd been seeing her all along. She was older than I was, with dark hair and large breasts. In my head she looks a bit like Monica Bellucci: exotic, aloof and sexy.

I deliberately walked by the shop more than once in the ensuing months, trying to catch a glimpse of her in her unflattering uniform polo shirt, stocking shelves or smiling at customers buying their groceries.

I spent a lot of time that autumn hating her quite determinedly, wishing upon her all sorts of misfortunes, while simultaneously hoping that Henry would come to his senses and take me back. (I did not, of course, blame him.)

I saw Henry in the flesh just twice after that. Once, in the cinema, holding hands with the woman who would later become his wife; I would recognise her in their couple's selfies online.

The second time, I saw him in a bougie supermarket in town. Not the bougiest supermarket, but expensive enough to be considered kind of posh. I was there – of course – for the freshly baked bread, the 'posh bangers', the chocolate chip cookies, always to be purchased in a bag of five and devoured immediately.

I was, at the time, the thinnest I'd ever been – the thinnest I would ever be – a detail for which I was immensely grateful. I was deep into my weightlifting obsession, eating only meat and vegetables six days of the week (on the seventh day she rose and in accordance with all disordered eating patterns, gorged herself on freshly baked bread and cookies). I was wearing a striped coat and my hair had been freshly dyed pink and he said hi and told me he'd seen me on the TV.

'You're doing well for yourself!' he said.

He looked almost the exact same as he had a decade previously: tall, dark hair, big smile, bright eyes. I wondered, fleetingly, if he regretted letting me go. I wondered if he thought, *Damn, I made a mistake.* It seemed important, somehow, for him to want me, in that moment, in the cold meats aisle. I guess I'll never know if he did.

I'm not glad we met, but I'm not sorry, either. I needed to get rid of something and he was willing to take it from me. In another world, I'd choose someone else – but in this one, I chose him, and there we were, in that semi-dark, damp spare room, sharing an experience that (thankfully) neither one of us will ever repeat.

Cian

I'm not sure where, exactly, or when I met Cian, who I would later come to regard as my first love, even as I grew older and less sure of what the word 'love' even meant. Was it a feeling or a decision? Perhaps a bit of both.

It feels quite like he was always there, on the periphery of my life, and me on the periphery of his – but there has to have been a day, a time, a moment. We were just so young and I find it difficult, now, to call to mind the details.

There was so much to remember, in those days of studying and exams and This Will Be The Year That Determines The Rest of Your Life pressure, that the precise moment I met my first real boyfriend – a boyfriend who took me to dinner in restaurants with candles on the tables and held my hand across the place settings and told me that he loved me – has faded into the abyss.

I don't even remember – and this is not a reflection on him, but on me – our first kiss. It was probably at a disco, the type of thing my parents still call 'a dance'. I wonder what teenagers today call it. Do they go to discos? Do they go to raves, or clubs, or do they merely go on 'nights out'?

I do, mind you, remember my first kiss, which was not with Cian. It was, though, at a disco – to the tune of Savage Garden's 'Truly, Madly, Deeply'. There are very few moments in my life that I could describe as belonging in a rom-com, but that moment, that kiss, I could imagine being immortalised in film. It would be an embarrassing coming-of-age film; the camera would zoom in on the awkward tongue-twisting of two teenagers who didn't know what to do, but it would be a moment all the same.

If that kiss was about anything, it was about ticking a box, about proving myself capable – not only of kissing with tongues, but of finding a boy who thought me worthy of kissing. The foreshadowing, in hindsight, is chilling.

I don't remember the first time I kissed Cian, but I do remember his scent. There are certain people – certain houses – who bear their aroma like a fingerprint, a tell-tale sign, and he was one of those. It wasn't a bad smell; at the time, of course, I drank it up. I was drawn to him by so many things, this pheromonal attraction just one of them.

I remember him asking me – to kiss? To go on a date? To be his girlfriend? I'm not sure – and that I said yes and that, for three years, on and off (I feel guilty, too, about this), we were, though most definitely not the hottest couple in school, by some degree the most committed.

We spent every lunchtime together. We went on a dirty weekend to Belfast, where we got in a taxi with a driver who told us that the one thing *not* to do in Northern Ireland was to get drawn into a conversation about Celtic v Rangers and that, if we did happen to have the misfortune to be asked, we should claim not to have heard of either team.

When, the year after school, I deferred college and took a job in the first ever Zara to open in Ireland – we took in a quarter of a million euro in the first day and at Christmas every staff member received a hamper of Spanish food and booze from the owner, who was, at the time, the richest man in the world – I spent two weeks training in the Regent Street store in London, and Cian came to stay with me. A fortnight was too long to be apart.

In London, I served Helen Mirren and existed in a permanent state of intimidation, not just at the sight of famous actors but at all the people I encountered. Londoners, no matter their age or background, just seemed infinitely cooler than Dubliners. Having Cian back in my hotel room, where he lounged all day and waited for me to come back to cuddle and take him to dinner, was a comforting taste of home.

Having got rid of my pesky virginity – another box ticked – before I met Cian, I slept with him two weeks after we became 'official'. By all rules of decorum and girls' magazines, it was too soon to sleep with someone, I knew, but I didn't care – I loved Cian, and he loved me.

I had never met anyone quite like him. He played

guitar and wrote poetry and listened to Counting Crows. His favourite song of theirs was a rather tuneless and melancholy lesser-known track called 'Anna Begins'. I thought this was a very deep choice for him to have made.

He seemed to find me endlessly fascinating, laughing at all of my jokes and taking my advice when I told him which colour to dye his hair, or which shade of trainers to wear to our school's graduation ball. (At the door, he was almost turned away by the venue's security team – his outfit was not black tie, apparently, but he had paid for his ticket so there was very little to be done; in any case, by the end of the night his shoes were, I'm sure, the least of their worries, as sleeping teenagers were hauled into taxis and buses, and vomit-filled plant pots were too numerous to count.)

The very first time we had sex – taking off one another's school uniforms, fumbling with bra straps and lying down on his parents' bed during a rushed lunchtime getaway – the condom split. We were both too inexperienced to notice at first, or even to consider that such a thing was possible. It wasn't until he withdrew that we realised he had broken through, the condom itself hanging uselessly around the base of his penis.

My dad used to say things like, 'There's no excuse for someone to get pregnant "accidentally" – condoms don't just fall off.' One could say this was the first moment that it struck me: maybe my dad wasn't always right?

To be perfectly honest, the split condom was a bit

of a thrill. I'd read about the morning-after pill in magazines, so I knew I'd have to go to a clinic, or to a GP – but I also knew that I couldn't possibly tell our family GP, the GP I shared with my mother, that I'd been having sex, and careless sex at that. And though I wasn't anti-abortion per se – I knew I definitely wasn't equipped or ready to have a baby – I'd had enough of an anti-abortion education to feel distinctly uncomfortable with the prospect of needing one myself.

A few months previously, we'd had a pro-life campaigner come into our religion class at school to talk to us about exactly what abortion was (murder), what it did (killed an innocent baby) and why it was a sin (see aforementioned murder).

Having been shown a particularly graphic video and encouraged to nod in agreement with our guest speaker, I asked if we would be having someone from the pro-choice side come to our school to have their say. After all, some of us were over eighteen – there was no Referendum on the horizon but, had there been one, we would have been old enough to vote. No, said Sister Imelda, our school chaplain, we would not be having someone from the 'pro-abortion' side come in to talk to us. Absolutely not.

So I went to a walk-in clinic in the city – and, though he offered, with a mildly terrified look on his face, Cian didn't come with me. It felt like the sort of rite of passage best done with one's best friend. In order to truly live out my *J-17* magazine fantasy, I would need to go with my gal pal, sit in the waiting room in stupefied silence and then ride the bus home quietly, in a sombre mood, thinking seriously about the baby that could have been.

We got the bus from the village and told our parents we were going window shopping. This alone should have been a big enough red flag for my mother, who knew well my inability to gaze passively at things I wanted.

The doctor in the walk-in clinic was about the same height as me, dressed in a three-piece suit and had a severe look on his face throughout proceedings. He took my blood pressure and gave me a perfunctory breast exam. I'd never had one before and felt incredibly awkward; he didn't explain why he was doing it and I didn't feel as though I could ask. I was, after all, here because of my own mistake.

He asked if I wanted to go on the pill and I said yes; it hadn't occurred to me that I should, but now that – I expected – Cian and I would be having regular sex, it seemed the only sensible option. I told him, suddenly realising that he'd thought I simply hadn't bothered using contraception, that the condom had split. He pursed his lips.

'Try not to have rough sex,' he advised. I didn't think we had been having rough sex and I was embarrassed at the idea that, after all this Judy Blume-reading, I had been doing it wrong. I never passed his advice on to Cian.

In a lot of ways, I think of Cian as the first person I slept with. He was the first man to go down on me, the first man to bring me to orgasm, the first man – honestly, still one of the few – to care about my pleasure, as well as his own.

That's not to say that he cared about my pleasure *over* his own. One of his favourite things to do was to ejaculate on my face. 'Can I come on your face?' he would ask as he approached his crescendo. I have always been very accommodating when it comes to men's sexual desires, so I would say yes – but afterwards, when he would toss me a towel and tell me to clean myself up, as if I had somehow diminished in his estimation, I would wonder if that was part of the allure.

I broke up with him several times.

It was as if his love for me felt like too much, too intense, like it would cover me up, smother me while I slept, bury me alive. But once we were apart and I had allowed myself space to breathe, I would miss the sheer weight of that love, holding me down. Being alone, with no one who loved me, felt like too little. I needed to be told that he needed me, that he loved me.

I regret it now, this back-and-forth, this inability to make up my mind. I never really stopped to think about how it made him feel; if I left him, only to feel the loss of his need, what did he feel as I walked away?

It's a need that has never truly left me. Sometimes, even now, I find it hard to separate my need to be loved with the truth of my love itself. Do I love the person that I'm with, or do I just love the fact that he wants to be with me? There is no denying that the knowledge of being desired, the truth of being loved, fills me up. I have never felt more whole than when I am half of a couple.

The last time I 'won' him back – the very last time I proved to myself, to him, to everyone, that he would drop everything for me – we'd been broken up for months. He'd moved on by dating Lynda, a girl who, to add insult to injury, had once been my best friend. I was convinced she had done it on purpose, had chosen this boy whose love had once been mine, and mine alone. She knew how much it mattered to me to feel that he wanted me, and she was trying to take that away.

A decade later, I would bump into Lynda on the street, exchange numbers and arrange to meet for a drink. Over bottled beers, she would tell me about a guy she met on Tinder. His name was Shane; she thought maybe I knew him from college. I did. (I had.) I realised then that she hadn't been chasing my ex-boyfriends, after all. We just had exactly the same taste in men. I felt bad, then, for all the years I had accused her of snacking on my leftovers.

Anyway, Cian was dating her when I decided that I needed him back. Again. Without his love for me, I felt unseen. We were at a party – actually, in the house of the boy who had been, for a short time, my pre-school boyfriend. We had held hands over the playdough table, smiled at one another across the Duplos. Ours was a small village.

I kissed Cian on the couch in the front room, sat on his lap, reminded him what it felt like to be with me, to have his tongue in my mouth, his hands in my hair. I sat astride him, ground my crotch against his, felt the moment his body remembered mine. He broke up with Lynda that day.

I broke up with him – for the last time – two weeks later. I felt bad about that, too.

More than ten years later, I found a letter he wrote me shortly after that, our final breakup. I was in college in Galway by then. We were still in touch, but sporadically. I have never been one for the 'clean break' people wax lyrical about; I find it hard to let go. I always have.

The letter was a lot of nothing, but it was five pages long and he was not an enthusiastic writer. I appreciate the effort of it now more, perhaps, than I did then.

I never told Cian this, in the years afterwards, but I thought he had come to visit me once. I saw a man getting out of a taxi in the courtyard outside of our student apartments – about Cian's height and build. He'd leaned into the back of the taxi and produced a guitar case. It couldn't be anyone but him.

I felt a rising sense of panic at the thought that he had come all of this way, cross-country, to try and win me back. I was pretty sure he would succeed; there is no way that I – faced with this irrefutable proof that he needed me, wanted me, loved me – could turn him down. We would end up back together and I would begin the countdown to our next breakup, torn between the ecstasy I felt at the knowledge of his devotion to me, and the stifling suffocation of his love.

To my relief, it wasn't him. We didn't see one another again for what, eight years? He met a girl he loved enough to move to Finland – of all countries – for, and he never came back.

I realised, when he got on that flight and became resident in another country, where he knew no one and didn't speak the language, that his love was just as obsessive as my need to be loved. We had been, in that respect, a potent combination: him, willing to do whatever it took for the woman he loved; and me, willing to do whatever it took to be that woman, who was loved that much.

It made me feel a little less special, but honestly? I also felt relief. It wasn't just me; I wasn't responsible. I had broken his heart, sure, but in a way it seemed as though it was destined to be broken.

When we next saw one another, Cian told me how well things were going for him. He was working for a multi-level marketing company (not, he stressed, a pyramid scheme, though a later court case would suggest otherwise) and full of Very Big Plans. He had met a very famous, philanthropic Irish musician (not that one – the other one) through a friend of a friend and they were going into business together. It sounded exciting.

He told me he'd heard I was doing well and that I looked great, and afterwards, we hugged. He smelled exactly the same as he had those many years before.

There was a moment where I thought I could have pulled him back in. I could have been loved again.

Cian

We could have talked about how ours was a puppy love that ended up as the real thing. Instead, I told him it was nice to see him. I wasn't lying.

Interlude: A Girls' Trip

I went to Gran Canaria on a girls' holiday, if it can be called that when there are just two of you, the summer after my year off, before I started university in Galway and moved away from the life I'd known up to then. We found a cheap deal, 300 quid or so for a shared bedroom in a three-star hotel in what was known as the Irish part of Gran Canaria, with a pool and a residents' bar and a 'lively programme of activities', and off we flew.

I had just broken up with Cian and was in a state of extreme melancholy that can only be fully understood by listening to the entirety of Avril Lavigne's sophomore album, *Under My Skin*. I was particularly enamoured with one song, 'Fall to Pieces', in which Avril sings, essentially, about wallowing. She does not want to be comforted (I did not want to be comforted); she just wants to sit and cry about her ex (I just wanted to sit and cry about my ex). I listened to it on repeat by the pool, with a baseball cap covering my eyes. I loved the idea of lying in this sunny paradise, watching people laugh and splash and swim and sunbathe, while I basked in my heartbreak and suffering.

My friend Laura – the one I'd stolen Henry from, the long-suffering friend who'd forgiven me and moved on and was now lying by the pool with me – was characteristically intolerant of my moping. She said things like, 'Well, if you decide you want to get back with him when we get home, we can worry about that then!' from the shelter of a beach umbrella, slathered in factor sixty, which gave her a pallid, unearthly sheen. It was like being advised by the Ghost of Christmas Past, except in thirty-degree heat.

Though I had declared, rather imperiously, as we boarded our plane, that this was *not* going to be a drinking holiday, it soon became clear, even to me, that Gran Canaria would never be anything *but* a drinking holiday to a couple of nineteen-year-old girls for whom this was the first trip ever taken without parental supervision.

On our first night, we'd gone out 'on the town' after dinner, all dressed up in our glad rags at 8 p.m., ending up in an Irish bar with a range of fiftysomething couples busy washing down their meat-and-two-veg dinners. We soon learned that Gran Canaria was a place where nights out started at midnight and ended at 5 a.m.; we started napping after dinner, rising once more at 11 p.m. to begin the beautifying process and head out.

Black Eyed Peas' 'Shut Up' was a reliable dance-floor classic then – I had a routine which involved spinning around the dance floor until I found a man facing in my direction, at whom I would thrust my palm and mouth the lyrics during the chorus. Those were the best of times, etc.

I kissed a boy on our second-to-last night, brought him back to our room – again, long-suffering Laura was left out in the cold – where he told me I had the most beautiful tits he'd ever seen. We had unprotected sex; he hadn't brought any condoms, which I thought seemed reckless, while of course I didn't have any because I hadn't intended on having sex with anyone. I was just going to listen to Avril Lavigne and weep.

The next morning, we saw him by the pool and said goodbye. I ordered us one final Smirnoff Ice – cool, sweet and refreshing – for the road. Laura took one look at me and asked, 'What happened to this not being a boozy holiday?' I'd changed.

I didn't want to get back with Cian after that. Something about this posh, blond English boy seemed to have exorcised all of those demons for good. We later became friends on Facebook and I realised that he had a girlfriend, a very shiny-haired girl who had a gorgeous smile and, crushingly, a great pair of breasts. So I guess he hadn't expected to have sex either.

Shane

Shane was a kind of stocky, sandy-haired 'lad' – not a boy, but definitely not a man – who was a year ahead of me in college. We were neighbours in my first year of student accommodation; our apartments were two doors from each other, and we first met outside his door, or mine, or somewhere in between.

I'm tempted to attribute my lack of precise recollection to the fact that, in spite of the emotional turmoil it wrought, ours was not all that significant a relationship, but I think it might just be that it wasn't that significant a moment. It wasn't like our eyes met across a crowded room and some sort of mating bond clicked into place; ours was not a love at first sight.

Shane had that certain confidence that all teenage boys seem to me to possess. He was self-assured and appeared not to have any insecurities – at least, none that he was stupid enough to reveal.

In a lot of ways, I was a pretty confident person, too – or at least good at giving that impression. I did worry sometimes that this confidence I was trying so hard to truly embody – nothing is sexier than confidence, I'd read in *More* magazine – came across as arrogance. Shane had no such qualms. When he made statements, it was in the style of an archaeologist who had just discovered the irrevocable proof of that very fact. There was no arguing with him (I wouldn't have dreamed of it).

This did not seem significant to me at the time, but Shane had the kind of facial hair that requires daily grooming: A carefully trimmed goatee, with no beard hair around it. A thin, short moustache. Craig David was still cool, so this kind of landscaped facial hair wasn't especially remarkable, but I am now very judgemental about a goatee. It is the surest sign of a man who freely makes the same mistake each and every morning, never stopping to think that he could, and should, make a different choice.

Of course, I fancied Shane immediately – I fancied everyone back then. I still do. When people ask if I have a type, I laugh and tell them I'm an equal opportunities heterosexual. They laugh, too. (They think I'm joking.) Shane was just another man with the power to make me feel wanted, to make me feel desirable, to make me feel attractive.

The timeline of that year is a bit jumbled in my memory, no thanks to the twenty-four-hour stretches I would spend in Shane's apartment with him and his housemates – Jason, Will and Cathal – playing *Grand Theft Auto*, taking breaks for pizza or to walk to Supermac's for burgers and chips.

I was there when they went into Galway city to

buy a house hamster, a cute little thing everyone fed (but nobody cleaned). I was one of the gang.

We first got together on a night out. It was fancy dress, I think, although I don't remember what we were dressed as. It is testament to just how determinedly I pursued this man that I even *went* to a fancy-dress night, something that I have not done since.

I remember kissing under strobe lights. I remember Shane taking me by the hand, suggesting that we go home. I remember him saying we shouldn't tell anyone, not wanting anyone to see. I don't remember finding that insulting, although in hindsight, of course, it serves as proof that he, like so many other men in their late teens, was a dickhead. I remember sharing a taxi, him acting as though we were going back to his apartment, as usual, to play *GTA*, me terrified that he would change his mind in the fifteen minutes it took us to get there.

When we got into my bedroom – I think my apartment was chosen because of the likelihood that the lads would be at his, and also due to the sheer stench of the hamster – I took off my own clothes. I knew what boys were like; they could barely manage a zipper, bless their hearts.

Shane was sitting on my bed, leaning back on his elbows. 'You're very confident, aren't you?' he remarked, seeming surprised.

'Should I not be?' I asked, feigning a bravado that I've never truly possessed.

I'm sure it will come as no great surprise to learn that he hurt my feelings. Boys were always hurting my feelings back then. I took every slight criticism deadly seriously. (I probably still do.)

Though it had absolutely no impact on my feelings for him, or my strong belief that this was the beginning of something wonderful, the sex wasn't very good. He came (did we use a condom? I hope we did, although honestly, knowing myself back then ... it's not guaranteed); I didn't. There was no mention of my orgasm, of any potential pleasure that I might have derived from the interaction.

To be honest, it was enough for me to know that he was turned on by me, that he wanted to have sex with me, that he wanted *me*. I didn't know then what I know now: that sexual desire and romantic desire are two very different things. One can exist independently of the other. I just wanted to be wanted, whatever form that took.

We had sex once more, after another night out with our group of mutual friends – a night out that I embarked on with the explicit purpose of hooking up with him again.

I have since read that the moment of orgasm is, for men, often the end, while for women it signifies a beginning. I thought we were starting something – but he, in hindsight, simply gave in to my determination.

My subsequent humiliation at Shane's hands was just another in a long line of boy-related (or, arguably, entirely self-inflicted) humiliations. I regret a lot of things, but allowing myself to be humiliated by men who shouldn't have held that power is pretty high on my list.

Shortly after our 'romance' began – while I still harboured hope of its developing into something greater – Shane began to see the girl next door. The *other* girl next door. The slim blonde whose flat midriff was always visible between the waistband of her skinny jeans and her worn band T-shirts. By the time I found out, they'd been together for weeks.

She was the type of girl who would trip and fall over in front of a group of people and laugh at her own misfortune until everyone around her was laughing too, tears pouring down their faces. I was the type of girl who would trip and fall over in front of a group of people and burst into tears, my cheeks burning with humiliation, a shame that spread through the group until no one knew where to look or whether to offer a hand to help me up.

I once tripped in IKEA, while walking along the painted footprints, diligently obeying the signposts that indicated which department you should stroll through next. I was with my then-housemate, Regan, shopping for glass tumblers and table lamps and, as always, on the lookout for a new houseplant to kill.

I rolled over my ankle, stumbled and landed on my hands and knees in the middle of an array of styled bedrooms. Regan looked away, his hands in his pockets. He began to browse the various wardrobe finishes. White? Light pine? Chestnut?

Later, I would ask him why he hadn't helped me. 'Oh, I find that kind of thing terribly embarrassing,' he confessed. 'I prefer to act like it hasn't happened.'

I think Shane and Regan would probably have that in common.

At some stage, both Shane and the (other) girl next door decided not to tell me about their romance. I'm not sure what they thought I'd do in response. Cry? Burn Shane's pile of old *Empire* magazines? Kidnap the hamster and keep him for myself? (He would've been better off, as it happens.)

When I eventually found out – I'd had my suspicions, and was asking anyone who'd listen if there was *something going on* between them, while hoping beyond hope that there wasn't – it was from my own housemate, who confessed that they were, in fact, together; that she'd known for a while; that everyone knew.

I was horrified. Not at the fact that Shane was seeing her, which, now that I knew the truth of it, seemed sadly inevitable, but at the fact that a group of people, people I thought of as my friends, had decided to keep this secret from me.

I felt pathetic, as if none of us had ever been friends to begin with. I was just the clingy hanger-on who had tricked a boy into thinking she was cool and laid-back, when the truth was precisely the opposite.

It's important to note that they were entirely and absolutely correct in their assumptions. I would not have taken the news well. (I did not take the news well.) In a way, the fact that I got to direct my anger towards the secret-keeping itself helped me – it would have been worse if I'd had to admit that I was just plain heartbroken. It's not easy to admit that, even now.

They stayed together for a few months, as I tried my hardest to feign insouciance. If I could stay super-friendly with the two of them, I could convince everyone – including myself – that I was, in fact, cool and laid-back; that it was no big deal; that I hadn't had my feelings hurt (it has taken me until my mid-thirties to realise that having one's feelings hurt is not a sign of weakness, but a sign of humanity).

'It was just sex!' I laughed. 'We're way too different to ever go out.'

Either I was very convincing or no one cared about my feelings, because I was soon let into Shane's confidence about his new romance. He told me when they first had sex (not, crucially, after a night out mere weeks into their acquaintance); when he told her he loved her. I pretended to be pleased for him. 'I just want you to be happy!'

The following year, we all moved out of on-campus student accommodation. We knew the lay of the land and we had friends now. We could find our own places to live. Shane and I saw each other around, but we weren't friends any more. We may have hugged at graduation, but if we did I don't remember it. I doubt he does either. I would be lying if I said I hope he's happy now (I wish him no ill will, but I have no investment in his emotional wellbeing) – but I do hope he's learned to hide his shock when women don't hate their bodies. I hope he's become a more responsible pet owner. Above all else, though, I hope he's lost the goatee.

Murph

There are certain people who, I think, we designate as 'safe' early on, before they've ever really earned it. There are friends of our parents, parents of our friends, boyfriends of girls we know through school or through choir or through friends of friends, around whom we don't see the need to exercise caution.

When I walk home at night, I carry a key between my index and middle finger, pointed outward like a knife.

But around these men, I leave my keys in my bag. Sometimes, I forget they're even there.

Murph was a friend of a friend – someone I knew, like Cian, from 'around'. He was slightly older than I was, maybe a year, maybe two. Some details seem less relevant than others. He was there the day a boy I knew sang the Beach Boys' 'I Get Around' as I walked by, the day after I had kissed a boy at a local disco, a boy who had then told his friends that I had 'great tits', adding a regretful, 'shame about the face'.

I can't remember whether or not Murph laughed – he was not the type to instigate a moment of derision like that, I don't think, but he wouldn't be the one to shut it down, either.

Murph was smart and funny – likeable enough to be on good terms with almost everyone, from the most popular to the least. He was confident, not in the kind of brash, obnoxious way some teenage boys are when they are full of their own intelligence and swagger, but just in a way that showed a certain self-assuredness, a comfort with himself. He had good comic timing, making witty quips at the right moment, which made him a welcome person in any group setting. I can see now that the talent he had was in punching up, rather than down – his laughs never came at anyone else's expense.

We became friendly through another friend, who was at the time dating a good friend of his. As a teen-ager, our social groups were tight-knit. Once you found your groove – whether that was with the girls on the basketball team or the girls who were in the choir (and yes, though the school was co-ed, the pri-mary social groups were almost always divided strictly by gender) – their friends became yours. It was the domino effect of friendships: make one, get three more without even trying.

At our school graduation ball I remember Murph asking if I was okay, giving a wry smile that sug-gested he knew the answer to the question. I was there with one of my closest girlfriends as my date, while Cian was with another girl who'd asked him during one of our off-again periods. Determined to give the impression of having The Most Fun, I drank ten shots of Tia Maria with a Baileys head (a Baby Guinness, as it's called) before dessert was served, and spent most of the night puking in the ladies' loos. Murph didn't try to save me. He wasn't the type.

We went on a date a few weeks after Cian and I had broken up for good – although, at the time, it didn't seem like a date. Murph asked if I wanted to go for a drink, just the two of us, and I was flattered that he would want to spend time with me, arguing with my sister that this was *not* a date because, '*God*, can guys not just want to spend time with girls?!' It felt as if to assume it was a date would be in some way ridiculous of me, not to mention vain.

It had never occurred to me to consider the fact that someone wanting to spend time with you is, in and of itself, lovely – sometimes just as much so as someone being attracted to you in a sexual or romantic way.

I knew, though, about two drinks in, that this *was*, in fact, a date. It wasn't just because he kept asking if I was over Cian – and gently teasing me about Cian's public displays of affection, his overt romanticism – but because he placed his hand on my leg and kept it there for the evening, each drink emboldening him to move ever so slightly further up my thigh.

When last orders were called, I was drunk. I rarely drank beer, except with boys I wanted to impress, and I was three pints in at this stage, buoyed by the alcohol, the bubbles causing me to burp, I hoped subtly, into my shoulder at regular intervals.

I had decided – probably, let's face it, halfway through my first drink – that I was going to sleep with Murph or, at the very least, go home with him and get 'handsy'. Quite aside from any other concerns, I fancied him a lot. Like I said, he was smart and funny – but he was also charming, and good-looking in the way that people of average attractiveness are elevated by their own confidence. I liked to imagine that I was attractive in the same way: maybe a four, looks-wise, but a solid nine once you got to know me.

In the pub that night, he leaned towards me after last orders were called, snaked a hand around my waist and kissed me like he'd rehearsed the move. I was (of course) impressed.

I'm still impressed now, especially when I juxtapose it with the many times I've kissed people, when I think of the awkward, charmless moves I've made. I would say that he knew what he was doing, but I think it was more that he just didn't worry about it. He wasn't the type of person to whip himself into a frenzy thinking about when or how or even whether to kiss someone. He just did it.

When we got back to his place, he was enthusiastic, but gentle. We kissed on his couch for what felt like hours. He snuck a hand up my top – then down my pants. There was an innocence to it that retains, even now, a certain charm.

This being an Irish home in the early noughties, now well past the hour of midnight, the heat was firmly off. The temperatures must have been in the low teens. As we kissed, I could see the soft clouds of condensation that made up our mixed breaths. If I'd had my glasses on, they would have fogged up.

I began to shiver and, again with that knowing look, Murph suggested we get into bed. I was drunk, tired and very, very cold and this sounded to me like a fab plan.

We had sex with the lights on, beneath the duvet and two blankets. I could still see the mists of our breath, batting against one another's cheeks, chins and lips. He was incredibly gentle, loving even, and it occurred to me then that he seemed to have *actual* feelings for me, which, I am ashamed to say, made me feel oddly uncomfortable.

I had been approaching this all as though we were friends who might have some kind of unexplored – at least, until this moment – sexual chemistry, whereas now I worried that he might actually be looking for something less to do with sex and more to do with romance.

Fresh out of my tumultuous three years on again and off again with Cian, I didn't feel like I could cope with anything, or anyone, too emotionally demanding.

Still, I remember turning my back to him and scooting close, wrapping his arms around me, trying to use his body heat to mop up some of the cold that seemed to have seeped into my bones.

'You're really cuddly,' he said to me, tightening his grip slightly around my midsection, leaning his head down to kiss my shoulder. 'I didn't think you'd be so cuddly.' He sounded delighted.

We went out again just once, this time on what could only have been described as a date, to a kind of hole-in-the-wall restaurant in Dublin city centre that I'd never heard of. It was Korean, and offered two menus: one for the Irish people who couldn't cope with the notion of noodles in clear broth, and the other for the Korean and, probably, broader Asian population who weren't afraid of a little spice and didn't need a potato side with every main course.

He had eaten there a few times, and so was au fait with the menu, insisting that we order from the non-Irish edition, pointing out the things he'd tried before. Crispy fried beef and squid and chicken, all in tapas-style portions, with sides of rice and crunchy green beans.

I was impressed by the kind of imperiousness of his ordering for us, probably because I'd never been to a restaurant with a dual menu system before and I was – though I'd have liked to consider myself a relatively sophisticated eater at that stage of my life – absolutely terrified of ordering something that in any way resembled ears, or feet, or any of the other many pieces of animal that I'd been led to believe were delicacies of the Asian world.

It was early when we wrapped up dinner, and I was headed home. Whatever serendipity had resulted in our being able to sneak an overnight stay past our parents the last time, tonight it was not to be and I was going home to Kildare, while he was meeting a friend for a drink before getting the bus back to his own house.

He walked me to my stop and waited there with me for the ten minutes or so it took for the bus to arrive. I had decided, at some stage over dinner, that I didn't really want to be more than friends – I liked him a lot, but there was something off-putting about how obviously he had been trying to impress me, enough to quell whatever amorous feelings I'd had for him on that last night in the pub.

There is a whole thesis to be written on this tendency to be put off by someone else's enthusiasm when, in fact, enthusiasm should be the absolute lowest bar for entry into any form of romance, but I am not the PhD candidate for that hard-hitting investigation.

Despite my having decided that this would be it as far as our romance was concerned, when he kissed me at that bus stop, I kissed him back. He had taken me out and chosen well from the menu and even insisted on paying for our meal, and a snog at the end of the night felt like the least I could do.

It was only when his hand began to migrate from my waist up beneath my top and inside my bra – at the bus stop! In not-quite-broad-daylight but pretty close! – and I shoved it back down, that I knew I was making the right decision.

I don't remember ever actually sharing this with him, mind you. I simply responded noncommittally to his texts – if I responded at all – and, after a few weeks, he seemed to get the message that I was not interested in pursuing things with him. I often wonder if he blamed himself for trying to squeeze my boob in public and, though I had determined to dump him before that moment, I hoped that at the very least he had learned not to do that to anyone else.

That wasn't, of course, the last time I'd see him. We had friends in common, and though I was in college a few hundred-odd miles away, nights out on the weekends I was home often saw us sitting with one another at a crowded pub table, or exchanging pleasantries as we lined up at the bar (me ordering alcopops or double vodkas with Coke, now that I was no longer trying to impress him with my own ideas about What Men Want Women to Drink).

When, one weekend, I decided to invite a group of friends to stay in my student accommodation and go out on the tear – I had four housemates who went home to their parents' each and every weekend, a fact for which I was incredibly grateful, relishing my weekends alone, with the run of the apartment – Murph ended up on the list, and half a dozen people rocked up to my door with sleeping bags and (I hoped) toothbrushes in tow.

It became clear to me early on, as we engaged in our pre-drinking in my apartment – imbibing just enough so that we wouldn't need to buy too many expensive drinks when we made our way to the club later that night, but not enough so that we could be denied entry for being clearly intoxicated – that Murph was going to try his luck with me tonight.

The flavour of it had changed a bit, though; he was being more outwardly flirty, less romantic in his pursuits. It felt as though he was of a mind that, as we'd slept together before, I might be as close as he'd ever get to a sure thing, which made me more determined than ever to keep my distance.

Something you should perhaps know about me is that I find the responsibility of coordinating a night out incredibly stressful. The wrangling of these people, for whom I felt responsible, having enticed them down to Galway with the promise of a Great Night Out, had given me a feeling of great worry and concern. I felt a bit like I was about to walk into a job interview – a pit in my stomach, acid-filled, gnawed at me all night long.

I was both right and wrong to worry. One of my closest friends got incredibly drunk. She was one of those people in whom, usually, you cannot discern any signs of drunkenness, but on this night she was stumbling in her high heels, slurring her words. She had met a young man she knew from school, the younger brother of one of her friends, and was pursuing him relentlessly – and literally – down the street, telling me, when I tried to corral her back towards the taxi rank and home, 'I *love* him! I'm *in love* with him!'

The following day, she admitted that she'd never considered him romantically before that night, nor would she ever again. His older brother was the one on whom she'd had a crush, and even that was the kind of thing that she had never dreamed of acting on. He had been on the debate team with her. 'It gave me a reason to look forward to debating!' she protested, a sentiment to which I could entirely relate.

Everyone else was at home, two asleep beneath blankets on the floor or on the couch, a few eating toast smeared with an unreasonable amount of butter at my too-small kitchen table, by the time I finally managed to wrangle her in the door with promises that she would see her one true love again.

I was exhausted. The adrenaline of panicking about everyone else's night had meant that the copious amounts of alcohol I'd consumed had little to no effect, and without the soft numbing impact of inebriation I had no more energy for entertaining, or mothering, or anything in between.

Somehow, I had managed to avoid having anyone sleep on the floor of my own room, so when I finally made it to bed, I was blissfully alone – until, mere moments later, there was a soft knock on the door. It was Murph. (Of course it was Murph.)

I opened the door. When he asked if he could come in, I said yes. When he asked if he could sleep in my bed with me, *I said yes* and, all along, I was thinking, *No, no, no*. I wanted to be alone. I wanted to *sleep* alone. I didn't want to be romantically involved with him any more, a fact of which I thought he was aware, yet here we were.

A lot of my decision-making – that night, but also, I think, in life – is influenced by what will be easier. It was easier to invite him in than to rudely (I thought) keep him out. It was easier to say yes than to risk the awkwardness of saying no. I wasn't afraid of him; I wasn't worried that he would get angry, or violent, just that he might be slightly irked or offended, that there would be some kind of scene caused and that I would be embarrassed.

I invited him in.

He asked, then, if I'd kissed anyone that night. I told him I hadn't. (I wonder, sometimes, if it would change anything if I had told him that I had, in fact, kissed someone else. Knowing now how possessive some men become when something they consider *theirs* is shared with someone else, I think it might have.) He asked if he could kiss me.

There is something romantic about this, as I write it down, but it didn't seem romantic at the time. It seemed like he was, as my mum would say, chancing his arm, and I was just so tired and so reluctant to engage in any form of conflict-adjacent resistance that I said yes, leaned forward, placed my lips on his, his lips on mine, and kissed him.

What happened next seems so depressingly predictable. He began to undress me and I said no, I didn't want to have sex, not tonight. We kissed some more. He tried again. It was a cycle that repeated for I don't know how long. Ten minutes? Twenty? An hour? I couldn't tell you.

We lay down on the bed and we kissed and I thought, *This is fine*, because, honestly, I like kissing. He was a good kisser. Ending a stressful night kissing a boy who clearly really liked me seemed like a pretty okay deal, even if it hadn't been in the plan.

He tried to undress me again, and again. I said no again, and again, until, at some point, I simply stopped saying anything.

It's hard, even now, to think about all of this, to quantify it somehow. I was kissing him, so that implies consent of some sort. But I did not consent, at least not verbally, to being undressed, to having sex. I did keep kissing him, and as he penetrated me, I thought, *It's easier to just let this happen than to keep saying no.*

I thought that letting someone have sex with me – as though I were an inanimate object, some *thing* that things happened to, rather than some*one* with her own thoughts and agency – was easier than being firm and telling him no and pushing him back out my bedroom door. Maybe it was; I'll never know exactly what would have happened if I'd kept saying no. Would there have been a magic no? The one that was one too many, that caused him to finally back off?

Afterwards, he kissed me on the forehead and left the room. That was the moment that I realised that he hadn't, in fact, come to my room to find a place to sleep for the night. He didn't even want to sleep there, with me; and he seemed to sense that, after what had happened, I would want to be alone.

We never spoke about it again, and I told very few people. Those I did tell were as confused as I felt. 'But you . . . let him? You didn't just tell him to leave?'

I felt worthless.

In the following weeks, whatever boundaries I had regarding sex and relationships came crumbling down. I went out to bars and nightclubs and I kissed whoever wanted to kiss me, and I went home with whoever asked me, and I brought home whoever wanted to come.

It wasn't until my sister asked me what I was doing – 'I'm worried about you,' she said, in a way that felt like genuine concern when it could easily have felt like shaming – that I realised I was coping with this incident by acting as if my body, and the giving and taking of my body, was entirely unimportant. Because if I could convince myself that it didn't matter, I could convince myself that night didn't matter, that it wasn't important, that nothing of consequence had happened and it wasn't a big deal. (Remember? Don't cause a fuss.)

I've seen him since – in the pub at Christmas; at a friend's wedding. We say hi to one another but I try not to engage in conversation. It's easier when I know it's coming; one day, I spotted him across the aisle in a fancy supermarket in Dublin and began to hyperventilate. I left without the expensive rainbow carrots I had come in search of. I don't think he saw me. Although I guess, like so much else, I'll never know.

Sean

In a weird way, if we hadn't ended up having sex in that shed outside his friend's house – with the pool table behind and a shelf of tools in front – Sean might have become, at least in my mind, the one that got away. Any time I thought about him, I would wonder whether or not he knew how much I fancied him, or whether or not my feelings were requited. As it is, I think about him un-fondly, as a man who fucked me and, frankly, forgot about me, all in the space of about fifteen minutes.

One thing that night has given rise to is one of my favourite stories about my dad – something I bring out to regale friends and family members with at regular intervals. It is a kind of illustration of my dad's courage, I guess you'd say, but also his absolute inability to think a plan through.

It was the night after Christmas, St Stephen's Night, the night Sean fucked me and forgot me in that shed. I remember because I had to pay a taxi driver double the usual fare to take me home to my parents' house afterwards.

Of course, at that point, they weren't expecting me. When I'd gone with Sean, after the nightclub closed, to the house party his friend was allegedly having, I'd texted my parents to say I wasn't going to be home. 'Staying in Eimear's!' I'd told them, knowing that they didn't know Eimear's parents well enough for my lie to ever be accidentally uncovered.

I'd been expecting that we'd have drinks and sit on sofas and maybe smoke some weed from a joint we'd pass around the room. I don't think I'd ever been at a party where there was more than one joint; that should tell you just how casual our drug use was. I hadn't been expecting that we would, instead, arrive before anyone else and head into the shed – a sort of repurposed playroom – and have sex on his friend's pool table, and that I would leave, in that overpriced taxi, before any of his friends even came to know I was there.

So, when I arrived home, drunk and slightly sore and even more disappointed, it wasn't straight to my room that I went, but to the bathroom, where I did the wee I'd been holding in for the thirty-minute taxi journey and promptly fell asleep, slumped over, my knickers around my ankles and my handbag clutched on my lap.

I woke up shortly thereafter – maybe five, ten minutes I think – but it was too long for my dad who, having heard the door open and slam shut, was growing increasingly concerned about the ensuing silence. He wasn't to know that his youngest daughter was asleep in the downstairs loo, or that, as he crept out of his room and stood at the top of the stairs checking to see whether he could hear anything going on below, I would wake from my slumber and decide it was time to head up those same stairs, to bed.

I still don't know what possessed him – I've asked many times – but he was entirely naked at the top of those stairs, his head peeking sideways around the corner, like a character in *Sesame Street* trying to hide behind a narrow tree. I looked at him; he looked at me. I laughed so hard I had to sit back down, on those cold stairs, hugging my bag as tears fell down my face. He didn't see the funny side until the following day, when he had got over the trauma of being awoken from his slumbers by what he thought was a burglar. A burglar with a fear of nudity, clearly.

I think about that moment a lot – more often than I think about Sean, thankfully – and wonder what would have happened if, instead of his drunk, sad, twenty-year-old daughter, my dad had found himself face to face with a festive robber. Would his nude form have called a halt to the thief's gallop? I guess we'll never know, but I like to imagine it.

Anyway: back to Sean. I look him up on Facebook every once in a while. It makes me feel uncharitably happy to see that he married a tall woman. In his wedding photographs, she stands a good three inches taller than he does. I know that some men don't care about this – and I truly believe that they shouldn't – but he's never quite struck me as someone who would be particularly progressive. And, in my sad experience, it is an extraordinary sort of straight man who gives zero fucks about being towered over by his partner.

I don't feel especially proud of myself, being happy that his wife is taller than he is. I wouldn't put it on my dating profile: 'Occasionally stalks exes on Facebook and feels smug if their partners are taller than they are.' If nothing else, it would be a waste of characters.

What I would really like to know, all these years later, is what it was exactly that caused me to have this ridiculous crush on this particular boy. I look at photographs of him now – yes, on the same Facebook page, and honestly, not that often, but really, if his Facebook page isn't private, can I be blamed?! No, I cannot – and I don't see the attraction. That's not an insult (although I admit it might sound insulting).

I can see how he would be exactly the type of man to do it, whatever 'it' is, for someone else. He just wouldn't do it for me any more. My taste now is different to what it was fifteen years ago. Go figure.

As a teenager, Sean had bad acne, although I don't remember meeting him until afterwards, when years of pimples had given him pockmarked skin, slightly red and shiny in places. I didn't find it off-putting. (He was not, in fact, the only acne-scarred boy I lusted over in my teen years. Maybe I was attracted by the idea that they knew what it was to suffer. They would, surely, be more compassionate and empathic as a result, or so I thought.)

There's a certain assumption that, I think, a lot of us hold as truth: that people who are ugly, or fat, or scarred, or in some way not beautiful, end up being nicer – because, without their beauty to fall back on, they have to try harder to be liked. That definitely wasn't the case with him.

What I do remember about Sean is that he was always laughing. His friends, the people around him, were always laughing too. He never seemed to be directing his laughter at anyone in particular; I didn't ever worry that he would turn to me and laugh, at least not in the way that would make me the butt of a joke.

That was – and is – an attractive quality to me, and very rare, especially in a teenage boy. I'd give him props for that. I hope he's managed to hold on to that sense of humour, the ability to make others laugh without finding someone to laugh at.

That night out – St Stephen's Night, in that night-club in the neighbouring town, the one we would have to call a cab to reach, then queue up to get into – was an annual tradition at that stage. It had opened a couple of years previously and we had gone every year since, as well as for birthdays and after Ladies' Day at the races, which took place nearby and had the advantage of being attended by people already in their clubbing ensembles, no day-to-night changes required (although I'm sure more than a handful of the attendees carried flat shoes in their bag, as is the Irish tradition).

I remember thinking, *There's Sean,* and then I remember thinking, *He has a girlfriend,* and then I remember him placing his hand on my bum and leaning in to press his body against mine and then I remember thinking, *They must have broken up,* and then I remember getting out of a taxi in his friend's house and him ushering me into the shed with a whisper because his friend's parents were asleep. I remember him telling me that.

I remember him penetrating me, first with a finger, and then with his penis – 'I don't have a condom, but I presume you're on the pill?' – with very little time or effort made to ease the transition. In his defence, that was a time in my life when the very pleasure of sex was the fact that another person was deriving pleasure from being with me. It's a through line that has followed me on every sexual adventure; even now, my sexual fantasies are rooted in the idea that I am wanted, that I am somehow giving pleasure to someone else. In my fantasies, it is the man who orgasms. I am always just the one being fucked.

I don't think it's any coincidence that my sexual fantasies revolve around my being thoroughly and absolutely objectified. I am the object of some man's – any man, a random man, a strange man – sexual desire. In real life, I don't think I have ever been that person. I don't think I will ever be that person. We always want what we can't have.

Sean fucked me that night the way I have fantasised about ever since – like I could have been anyone, like he barely knew my name, like the object of the exercise was for him to reach orgasm inside me and then to pull out, quickly and thoughtlessly, as if I was an old sock he had just used to mop up his cum. I am somehow thrilled by the idea that someone could want me, physically, without having any interest in me, as a person – perhaps because I have never thought of myself as someone whose physicality is their main draw.

I remember him saying to me, right after, while I was still facing away from him, while his sperm was dripping down my leg and he was breathing heavily on to my shoulder, 'I feel bad about my girlfriend.' I remember, clear as day, that I responded, surprised but also not surprised, 'Please don't try to make me feel bad; she's not *my* girlfriend.' And I remember him saying to me, as he stepped his body back and away from mine, as I began to feel the cold chill of that December night enveloping me in that unheated shed, 'barely dressed!' as my mother would have said, 'Don't be such a bitch.'

I didn't feel bad about his girlfriend then – I don't feel bad about his girlfriend now. I hope she's not the woman he ended up marrying, because when I scroll through his wedding photographs, I think I could quite like her, this smiling, taller woman Sean ended up married to.

I do feel bad that I let him fuck me in that shed; after that, I always demanded soft furnishings or, if it was to be a shed, that it would at least be the shed belonging to the man I would be having sex with. It's important, I know now, to have *some* standards.

I feel bad that I spent almost €50 on getting a taxi home, when I could have shared a cab with my friends and avoided the whole sorry ordeal – the pool table and the sperm and being called a bitch by a man, moments after he had come inside me. I feel bad, too, that I woke my dad up, but only a tiny bit, because it really is one of my favourite memories of him. I guess I have Sean to thank for that, if nothing else.

Tommy

Once, on holiday in Milan, I ran into a friend of a friend. Standing in the plaza of the Duomo, Milan's central cathedral, surrounded by tourists, I marvelled at how we – two Irish people who shared a mutual friend – had managed to bump into one another here, of all places.

There are some people whose shadows we can never get away from, whose footprints we can never outrun. The country feels too small, the communities too claustrophobic. But there are others we somehow never bump into, whose paths never cross with ours, for whatever reason.

There is a man I knew from secondary school, and dated for maybe six months in total, two years or so after we graduated. He was still a boy then, really, although now he is a man. He is married, he and his wife have two children, boys, whose smiling faces I can see through their not-very-private social media feeds. I look every now and then; I want to see what they're up to, what's new in their lives. It bothers me that I'll never know whether they do the same to me, to my social media profiles. I would like to hire a Lisbeth Salander character to hack their iPhones and to alert me whenever they searched my name. (If they never search my name, I would like her to lie. A lie can be a kindness.)

I met Tommy at school and, in what is becoming a common thread – an uncomfortable narrative I would very much like to leave behind, thank you very much – he first dated my friend Hannah.

I was not particularly interested in him to begin with – honestly – despite the fact that he was new and therefore mysterious and, crucially, interested in someone else. I would like to caveat this entire tale with the disclosure that Tommy was not then (nor is he now) a mysterious man. He is straightforward. If he was a breakfast food, he would be oatmeal – maybe some sort of kids' oatmeal that comes with a hidden surprise, like the bike reflectors I once collected from within the packet of my Kellogg's Frosties. A bike reflector would be a good surprise for his particular oatmeal pack: fun, but mostly practical. (That is to say: he made a lot of jokes, not all of which were good jokes. But, like I said, we were young.)

He and Hannah broke up one day, very much out of the blue. They had been so in love, we had thought. But as it happens, it was she who was in love. It was she who had been invested in the potential future of their romance, not he.

I feel, now, like I should tell you about the nature of mine and Hannah's relationship. It somehow seems important to clarify that, though we were in the same friendship group, we were not best friends. We rarely spoke on the phone; if we texted one another, it was in the context of someone else's birthday, or someone else's plans. Hers was not a confidence I was allowed into.

But really, that's an irrelevance. I didn't need some special, access-all-areas pass to know that Hannah's heart was broken. I didn't need a nightly phone call to know that it would take her longer than two months to get over this, her first love. I didn't owe her any special loyalty, but we were both teenage girls in the same school, in the same group of friends who ate lunch together, comparing warm sandwiches taken out of hard plastic lunch boxes, sharing crisps and swapping chocolate bars. I didn't – and yet, I did.

The night Tommy and I first kissed, I had no inclination that I would be kissing him. I had no desire to kiss him; I hadn't thought of him 'in that way' ever before. As I look back now on half a lifetime of dating, of relationships, it is striking to me how many romantic relationships started with an advance from a man, an advance that was received as a compliment. It was as if knowing that a man desired me made me automatically feel I should desire him back – or that the very fact of his desire was enough to elicit reciprocity from me.

The concept itself is not new; children, after all, learn to mimic the behaviours of their parents, of the adults around them, during a stage in development known as mirroring. They smile because we smile;

they look into our eyes because we started out by looking into theirs. There is a certain positive reinforcement in having a smile, or gaze, returned.

In any case, it happened on a night out – along with another incident which, at the time, was insignificant. As I grew older, though, and began to write down my experiences with men and their hands, touching things that were not theirs, it was given a certain weight.

I was in a club in Dublin we used to go to when we wanted to dance.

Upstairs, it was all glass and high-shine metal (this was a pre-recession golden age of sorts), while downstairs was darker, no less shiny but somehow with more of a disco vibe. The dance floor lived downstairs, as did the loos. We would start upstairs, drink a cocktail or two – or as many as we could afford – before moving on to spirits 'with a dash of lime'. The dance floor was never to be stepped on to before midnight and, even then, only for the right song: Christina Aguilera's 'Dirrty', or Usher's 'Yeah!'

It must have been past midnight because I was on the dance floor, busting my signature moves. I was a big fan of the musical mime – I have a great talent for remembering song lyrics and an even greater talent for interpreting them with very basic and slightly comical gestures, although at the time, I definitely thought I was being sexy.

Eric Carmen's 'Hungry Eyes' was conveyed with a combination of tummy-rubbing and eye-pointing, always with a very dramatic, unblinking stare. Holly Valance's 'Kiss Kiss', well . . . you get the idea. (Songs like Tatu's 'All the Things She Said' or Kylie Minogue's 'Slow' prohibited any kind of miming due to their difficult tempos, and so involved writhing and running one's hands up and down one's body for as long as one could without feeling awkward, twenty-two seconds max.)

I can't remember the song that was playing as I walked from the dance floor back upstairs to where my friends were – we were a mixed-gender group that night, which meant populating the upstairs area: the boys couldn't be too close to the dance floor in case it looked like they were dancing. A man I didn't know, standing next to his friend, stopped me as I manoeuvred through the crowd, said something I didn't quite catch.

'Sorry?' I asked. Why am *I* always sorry? I wasn't the one asking for *his* attention.

'Are your tits real?!' he asked, pointing at my boobs, resplendent in a low-cut black vest top, one of many 'going-out' tops I had in my arsenal, perfect for pairing with bootcut jeans and a pair of pointy-toed leather boots with a stiletto heel. (Having always had enormous calves, I have always found it difficult to find knee-high boots that would fit – this pair were made of a stretch leather, rather than stiff, and fitted perfectly, with the result that I bought them in two colours and wore them on every night out between 2001 and 2005.)

I responded straight away, and indignantly (if not with a modicum of pride): 'Yes!'

It didn't occur to me, at the time, to tell him to

mind his own business, or even to ignore him. I guess women are good at answering men when they speak to us, at trying not to make them angry even when they have, quite rightly, made us angry.

He didn't say anything else, then, just reached out with his hand and grabbed my right breast, squeezing it roughly, as if to check for himself. I doubt he would have known what he was feeling for, but he was determined all the same.

I walked away from our encounter feeling shocked and outraged, both at the sheer audacity of his public groping and at my own ineptitude. Why hadn't I said something? Why hadn't I slapped his hand away? I had basically *let* it happen. And was it my top? Maybe I was asking for it!

I went back to the group and told them all about 'this lad who grabbed my tit'. I didn't know then to call it what it was: sexual assault. It didn't strike me to report this man to the bouncers, to ask for him to be removed. It didn't occur to me that this man, who clearly thought himself entitled to women's bodies, might have been a danger to anyone else. I was just – as my mother would say – flabbergasted at what had transpired.

I told the boys with a kind of breathless incredulity. 'Can you—' I panted '—believe it?!' Tommy was the first to react, drunkenly – he seemed always to be drunk, from the moment we arrived in a bar or club to the moment we left – by announcing he was going to 'kill this lad' and stumbling, rather non-threateningly, down the stairs.

I ran – a precarious activity any day, never mind in bootcut jeans and stilettos – and stopped in front of him, placing my hands on his chest as if pushing the gallant hero back from the fray. It was very dramatic, an aspect I enjoyed a lot. He pushed against me slightly, as if to argue, and I pushed back, as if to say, 'I'm not backing down.' Then our eyes met and we were kissing, his mouth on mine, his hands in my hair, on my face, on my back, pulling me closer to him with each breath.

As first kisses go, this was it. This was the first kiss I had always wanted – where the orchestra surges and the birds sing and the background fades away and all that is left is you and him and the inevitability of your love. I had never thought of him before now, but this was not the type of kiss that *just happened*; this was not the type of kiss that meant nothing.

I wasn't exactly writing our wedding vows then and there, but I was convinced that this was the start of something incredible. It was not the type of kiss that would be left as a lone, isolated memory. 'That one night we kissed' – the kind of embarrassing, drunken mistake that we would laugh at in the pub in a few weeks' time.

We kissed for what felt like hours before separating, doing a loop and rejoining the others upstairs. No one asked where we'd gone, or whether we'd been together; it wasn't the kind of place where you kept close track of your friends, and besides which, we weren't the two people anyone would suspect of running off for a make-out session by the stairs. As a coupling went, we were beyond unlikely; like I said, it had simply never come up. I had never spoken about him in a romantic sense and, I realised much later, he clearly hadn't spoken – or even thought – of me that way either.

I was at university in Galway but it was spring coming into summer; I would be home for two weeks on the Easter break, for another three when term-time ended, a 'study break' designed to prepare us for the upcoming end-of-year exams. (I would do okay, in the end, in everything except psychology, through which I would scrape with a 40 per cent. I hadn't realised psychology would have so much to do with biology; I just wanted to know why people thought the way they did and, ideally, to learn their secrets.)

We would spend a lot of time together early that summer, either alone, listening to James Blunt's *Back to Bedlam* in his car, or with friends, fishing on the banks of the Grand Canal or drinking pints (which I was back to pretending to like) in the local on a Friday night.

In my recollections of our romance – which seemed longer, but only lasted about three months – my parents were away a lot. I think the more likely truth of it was that they were at work. He had got a job straight out of school and worked shifts; I was 'studying'. We spent a lot of time at home, having sex or watching movies.

Tommy put his thumb in my bum once. There's

just no great way to say that, is there? We'd been watching a movie and had started kissing, then paused it – I always find it too distracting to have sex with something on in the background. We were having sex doggy-style, me kneeling on the sofa and him behind me, when I felt his thumb, slick from what I can only suspect was his own saliva, entering my anus.

'Did you just put your *thumb* in my ass?!' I asked. He seemed sheepish, but laughed. 'Eh . . . yeah.'

I didn't have an issue with the fact that I had received an un-forewarned digit up the bottom – I was just perplexed at his choice of digit. If you were trying out bum stuff for the first time, I thought, wouldn't you start with the index finger or, if you were really trying to play it safe, the pinky? The thumb seemed like an odd choice.

Over a decade later, I expect my sexual partners to ask me before doing something entirely unexpected in bed, especially if it's something we've never done before. There was a time – a time when I was binge-ing Louise Bagshawe books and thought passionate, against-the-wall snogging was the height of romance – when I fantasised about being with a man who could flip me from missionary to doggy without so much as a 'by your leave', but now the idea of a man taking control with such a blatant disregard for my own preferences leaves me cold.

The thumb-up-the-bum wasn't a turning point in our relationship, as such – rather, things were brought to an unnatural pause by my going to Milan for ten weeks, to live with my sister and practise my Italian. I had decided that it, and English, were the subjects I would keep on for my second year in college and my sister had organised for me to work four nights a week at her favourite bar, which seemed too good an opportunity to pass up.

I don't remember that we kept in touch. I never gave him my Italian number and he wasn't the type to send long, loving emails – besides which, we had only been seeing one another 'casually'. While in Milan, I would go on several dates with a beautiful Mexican man named Poncho (yes, really), who wore a beaded coral choker and had his hair cut in a mullet. I was sure Tommy wasn't keeping himself for me while I was away. A mutual friend kept me updated with how he was and what he was up to. He had drunkenly told her, she confided in long, detailed emails, that he was really missing me. She said she'd never seen him like this about anyone.

When I got home, after ten weeks of tanning and drinking and shopping and eating focaccia and, oh yes, learning Italian, there was a night out arranged. Tommy would be there, along with an assortment of friends. I imagined a kind of reworking of our first kiss – a moment of impact, of inevitability, when we would come together from across the room.

That moment did happen, in a way – but with John, another friend of ours, who ran over to me the minute he saw me and scooped me up into a bear hug. 'You look *great*!' he told me. I knew I did; I was tanned and had lost weight, removed the lip ring I'd thought cool and edgy but which, I'd realised, gave me a sort of angry, tough look. Tommy simply nodded hello to me and turned back to his drink.

If I was upset at my reception, I never told him. We hooked up a few more times after that, but there was less James Blunt and fewer movies. He came over to my house once or twice, when my parents were out, and we had sex on my bed. I could feel him drawing away from me and so I pulled out all the stops, doing all of the things I thought boys liked, gazing into his eyes while giving him a blow job and making noises like it was somehow bringing me to orgasm, too.

Then, one day – kind of as quickly and as unexpectedly as it had started – it ended. He came over to the house – I thought for sex, which I would have characterised more as 'spending time together', though it really was just sex – and told me it was over. 'I just don't want to do this any more,' he said, as if 'this' was just a way to pass the time, a way to fill the summer days before the clocks went back and the nights got darker and we all began spending more time at home, counting down to Christmas.

As you can imagine, I didn't take it well.

In all, we had been seeing one another for three months or so – and yet, for the following six, I spent every drunken moment (in my late teens and early twenties, I had a lot of those) texting him, asking him what had gone wrong. I would call his phone at two in the morning and ask him where he was, barely able to make out his response.

The end – for me, at least – came in February 2006,

at my twenty-first birthday. He was there, of course, because all of my friends were, and whether I liked it or not, he was included among their number.

I had demanded that my parents pay for a shindig in a local pub – a pub, I should add, that I had never been to before and have never set foot in since – and pay for ridiculous things like a DJ and a finger-food buffet. I asked them recently why they allowed this, and my mother seemed taken aback. 'Allowed it?!' she scoffed. 'You wouldn't hear of anything else! You had! To! Have! The! Pub! Twenty-first!' she told me, banging the table between each word for effect.

At 1.28 a.m., the DJ played the Irish national anthem, a distinctly country tradition that I found twee and embarrassing. I, having specifically asked the DJ, earlier, *not* to play the national anthem, stomped around the dance floor as party attendees stood to attention, one hand over their hearts as a mark of respect. I can still remember the look of disgust on my father's face as we locked eyes right at the moment I downed someone else's drink, a delightful discovery made during my moment of anthem-related rebellion.

Tommy had just moved house to a three-bedroom in the 'burbs, a mere ten-minute taxi journey away, and word in the pub was that the after-party would be held there. I'm not sure where this rumour origi-nated, but if it meant the opportunity to continue celebrating the birthday girl – me! – at Tommy's house, of all places, I was in.

I met him on the stairs as we all filed out. My boots made negotiating the long staircase difficult, and I was holding on to the bannister with a sort of grim, drunken determination. He had been walking down ahead of me and, upon hearing the tap-tap of my heels, turned around.

'Hey,' he said.

'Hi!' I replied, chirpily. (I was deep in denial about the multiple late-night phone calls I'd been making, and *always* deleted my text history after a drunken night out, so as to protect myself from past me's mistakes, so I was being chipper and Totally Normal.)

'You know, I really think . . . I miss you,' he said, in a drunken mumble.

I didn't allow his words to halt my gallop.

'It's a bit late for that,' I said, in a tone that wasn't meant to be unkind. Then I walked past him and out the door, thinking, *Now, you just think about that until we get to your house and then we'll make up and get back together and live Happily Ever After.*

Of course, nothing ever goes to plan – especially if your plan has been made at an especially drunken moment, and no one else knows about it.

Tommy never made it back to his house. A small group of us – maybe six or seven – stood, shivering, in his driveway, as I called him repeatedly, begging him to tell me where he was.

'I don't know!' he slurred. 'I'm in a taxi! I'm going home!'

Eventually, he stopped answering. His phone went straight to voicemail. People began to call their own taxis. I went home with another friend, weeping loudly in the back of the car.

It turns out that Tommy had gone home to his old house – he was in the process of moving into his new place and was between both, and though he knew that people were coming back to his, he claimed he had got confused and ended up at the wrong one. He texted me the next day to apologise for the confusion. 'I hope you had a good night.' I didn't write back.

We never spoke about it after that – about the moment on the stairs, or about us.

Poncho

I spent the summer between my first and second years of college in Milan, living with my sister Beatrice in the one-and-a-half-bedroom apartment she shared with her friend Julie on Via Mario Pichi. It was a kind of greying street with the same industrial feel shared by so much of Milan, where a surge of apartment buildings had been built in great haste after the war, to respond to a surge in industry that, it was hoped, would reverse the country's fortunes.

My sister's bedroom doubled as our living room. Each morning, after she and Julie had gone to work, I would take the sheets and duvet off the futon and stash them in the linen closet, folding the mattress up into a low, three-seater sofa and opening the French doors that led on to a small balcony.

I had decided to go, ostensibly, to practise my Italian – but mostly to spend time with my sister, who had moved abroad two years previously, upon completion of her degree in fashion design. I didn't know it then, but she would never come home, moving next to Paris, then New York, Dallas and, eventually, to Fort Wayne, a former military city in the American Midwest.

Bea had set me up with a part-time job working a few nights a week in a small bar called Cape Town, right by Milan's central canal system. The owner, Sergio, was a slightly rotund Italian man who reminded me of every Italian man in every Disney cartoon I'd ever seen, except that he was younger, maybe in his mid-thirties, and wore Dolce & Gabbana sunglasses.

Work at the bar was a baptism of fire. My Italian, which had been *eccellente* in Ireland, was now pathetic. It took me several repetitions to take down anyone's order, and it was a pretty regular occurrence for groups of Italians, never famed for their patience or compassion, to demand another waitress.

I was not allowed to work behind the bar – something about the barwoman, Silvia, being the only one qualified to mix drinks – so I spent my time out front, taking orders and clearing glasses and laying out the *aperitivi*, an amazing Italian tradition where you get free food simply for being in the right place (a bar) at the right time (between six and eight in the evenings).

My being Irish was not as much of a novelty with the Italians as I thought it might be, although any American visitors were thoroughly thrilled. They were delighted, too, I think, at the fact that there was no tipping culture in Italy, and would use this as an excuse to spend hours in the bar, demanding drink after drink after drink, and leaving nothing but coppers behind for your troubles.

The most I made in tips in any one night was €1.50, not enough to get a taxi back to my sister's apartment.

In any case, I made it my nightly habit to walk home – just one of the many examples of my being incredibly reckless (and stupid) in my youth. A taxi would set me back the guts of a tenner, and cut into my evening's earnings so much that it almost made working pointless. Plus, I was always a bit hyper after my evening in the bar. Once the customers had cleared out, we would each have a drink – I would drink straight whisky with ice, mostly because I felt it reinforced the idea that Irish people can handle their drink – and then, when the place had been locked up, I would walk the thirty minutes home along the quiet, dark Milanese streets.

Beatrice even offered to pay for a taxi home for me each night, an offer I was too proud to take her up on. Besides which, my daily walk – thirty minutes there and thirty minutes back – was compensating for the six tonnes of focaccia I was managing to hoof into myself each week, slathered in oil and chased with a fistful of olives. By the time I got home, I'd be sweaty and exhausted and fall into bed next to Bea, trying not to wake her as I slid between the sheets.

I met Poncho in my first week working at Cape Town; he worked in the bar next door, which felt fancier than our bar by virtue of its having fabric napkins and individual candles on each table, but it was never busy, while Cape Town heaved with regulars from 10 p.m. onwards. He was Mexican, in

Milan to work and earn some money with his friend Pierre, a tall, handsome twentysomething with an impressive afro and an array of stylish, albeit filthy, trainers.

Poncho wasn't his real name, he told me, but a nickname; Pierre wasn't his friend's real name, either. I don't remember if I ever found out what their mothers called them; it didn't seem important. The whole summer felt like a temporary state of being, an interlude between acts, where we were all free to be entirely different people leading entirely different lives.

We got to know one another in gaps between customers, usually from eight to ten, after the post-work crowd had guzzled enough *aperitivi* to last them till dinner, and before the seasoned drinkers arrived for their serious nights out. His English was good, but I wanted to speak Italian – it would be weeks before I'd realise that he was speaking a kind of Spanish–Italian hybrid. While I thought I was perfecting my Italian by speaking to this skilled linguist, he was in fact polluting it with bad pronunciation, placing the emphasis on the wrong parts of the wrong words.

His mullet hairstyle was short all over with a tiny ponytail to finish it off, and he wore a beaded choker made of tiny shells. His skin was smooth and always warm to the touch; he smiled all the time. When I was around him I felt as though his warmth rubbed off on me, like I might suddenly be the kind of fun person to attract a handsome Mexican adventurer.

I had a crush on him for weeks before anything happened, hatching plans to get chatting to him after work and ask him if he wanted to get a drink or suggest getting dinner. But his bar closed before ours, always; our customers would hang on, waiting to chat to Sergio or Silvia, knowing that such a conversation would inevitably be accompanied by a free drink.

When we eventually did get to talk to one another outside work, it was by chance; I was at Cape Town on my night off, taking advantage of Sergio's generosity to drink discounted caipirinhas with Bea and Julie. He knew, I think, that we, being Irish, would drink more than the two drinks Italians tended to average – he could discount our drinks by 20 per cent and still make more of a profit than he would on another group taking up the same amount of space.

After three drinks, the waitresses – my workmates and kind-of friends, although we did not stay in touch after that summer – would ask if we wanted the bill, and we would laugh. They were amazed at my capacity for alcohol as much as they were at my willingness to spend half my week's wages on a single night out. But, I guess, they'd never been to Dublin.

I was there that night when Poncho got off work. Bea and Julie went home, or to another bar, I'm not quite sure. I went with Poncho and Pierre, who I had got to know from his regular visits to Poncho's place of work, to a club on the Naviglio, about five minutes' walk away. I was wearing low wedge sandals I'd bought in my favourite shoe shop on the Corso di Porta Ticinese; I didn't think to mention it when the cork inner began to bring the soles of my feet out in blisters.

Pierre left the club before us. Poncho and I were flirting outrageously, dancing and smoking – you could do that, then – in the middle of sweaty crowds of people. When we finally broke free of the club itself, we kissed on the street outside, his face illuminated by the light of a lamp that had seen better days, paint peeling off the post.

Poncho lived in a shared apartment, he told me; he and Pierre shared a room. I, sharing a bed with my sister, was clearly not in a position to take him home to mine, so we set about trying to find a hotel. It didn't seem to occur to either of us that we could kiss and say goodbye, that he could go back to his place, and I to mine, that we would see one another the following afternoon.

We walked around Milan for what felt like hours. That summer was hot – at night, it dipped to lows of twenty-odd degrees which, to an Irish person, is beach weather. I took off my shoes and walked, clammy-footed and drunk, around the city after Poncho, who knocked at each and every guesthouse we saw, asking if they rented rooms by the hour.

We were both broke – I'd spent all my money on caipirinhas and he, I would later learn, was getting paid a pittance as he didn't have a work permit and had no way of asserting his rights as an employee.

When we finally did find a hotel that rented rooms *a ore*, the sordidness of the whole thing became startlingly clear. I felt as if I were watching a horror movie through a fish-eye lens – the dame behind the counter, lipstick on her teeth, shrewd eyes heavily lined in black eyeliner, asked for the money up front.

'Let's just go back to yours,' I told him. 'We'll be quiet.' I imagined Pierre sleeping in a bed far across the room, snoring gently beneath cotton sheets.

The reality, of course, was far worse. Poncho was living in a sort of old warehouse that had been converted into a labyrinthine mess of bedrooms with what looked like scaffolding and old sheets, hung from the ceiling. Mattresses lay on pallets in every corner; one person's 'room' was a foot away from their neighbour's, separated by these makeshift curtains suspended from iron pipes.

There must have been 200 people in the place, each in a space about eight by four feet. The kitchen was shared – a fridge, microwave and a rickety sink, rust gathering at the edges. I didn't ask where the bathroom was; I decided I could hold it.

When we finally made it to his 'room' – we passed through several curtains, stepped over the sleeping bodies of, I guess, his housemates – I realised why he'd been reluctant to bring me home, if you could call it that.

Pierre was a foot away from us, on a tiny mattress against a concrete wall. They had one lamp between their sleeping areas. At the end of their bed was a suitcase, making a de facto table. I spotted a pile of clothes under Pierre's bed, two pairs of shoes tucked neatly beneath his sleeping torso.

It did not occur to me, then, to go home; I felt as if it would have been insulting to Poncho, like I was turning my nose up at his living arrangements. Not only that, but I would have led him on a wild pussy chase around Milan, promising him sex and then turning tail as soon as I realised this was not the Four Seasons of my dreams.

We had sex quietly, our bodies slick with sweat. I don't remember ever having been as hot, either before or after, as I was in that combined space, soundlessly straddling Poncho, who whispered things in Spanish (the languages were so similar to my untrained ear that I thought, at the time, it was Italian; it was only later, when I told him that I felt my Italian was improving, that he revealed that he and Pierre spoke Spanish to one another, and, mostly, to me).

I convinced myself that Pierre was sleeping the whole time; he didn't make a sound, after all, but I realise that his was a veritable Sophie's choice.

Upon waking the following morning, Poncho accompanied me home. We held hands on the metro and he kissed me goodbye at my door, told me he'd see me at work. It was easy, straightforward.

The rest of the summer, we spent as much time together as we could – usually after dark. During the day, I would sleep until noon and then take myself to the local pool for a few hours to read my book and work on my tan. At work, I would give him coy glances and, afterwards, we would find a late bar to have a drink in.

When Bea and Julie went to Sicily for a week,

Poncho came and stayed with me in their apartment. Once, after a late night drinking wine with Pierre and a Spanish girl he'd met, I allowed them to sleep in Julie's bed. I was racked with guilt the following morning, bundling up her bedsheets and taking them to the laundrette to have them washed, dried and replaced before her return. Julie and I were friendly, but I was, ultimately, Bea's little sister – openly taking advantage of her hospitality that way was out of the question.

When Bea and Julie got back from their vacation, they would invite Poncho over at weekends and the four of us would eat dinner on the terrazzo. He was there the night of their going-away party – once the summer was done, they were both moving to Paris, to take up jobs with a well-known French fashion house – and, as people mingled and clinked glasses in the living room, I went down on him in the loo. He told me I was amazing; I believed him.

When I'd told him they were leaving, he'd asked who was moving into their apartment; he, Pierre and the Spanish girl whose name I never learned were looking for somewhere to live. Bea introduced them to her landlord and he agreed to hand over the lease.

I like to think his life was better for having met me.

When my very last week in Milan arrived, towards the end of July – Bea and I were flying home together, to go to my cousin's wedding, then Bea was coming back to Milan to pack up her things and move, with Julie, to Paris – I suddenly lost interest in the entire endeavour, Poncho to boot. I began slacking at work, leaning over the counter and chewing gum, like a bored teenager in an American rom-com.

My friend back home had told me that Tommy couldn't wait to see me when I got back, and I suddenly felt horribly guilty. I couldn't wait to see him either, but I had a Mexican boyfriend here, too – what kind of person did that make me?

It felt as though my summer was coming to a close – figuratively, although, going back to Ireland's dull, damp weather, perhaps literally too – and Poncho's would carry on without me. He would move into a nice apartment and have his own room to sleep in, even if he did have to fold up the futon every day in order to have a functioning living room. I would go home and back to my old life, to a man who wouldn't be seen dead wearing a necklace.

I began to detach in what is now, clearly, a pretty cruel fashion. I was too busy, I told him, to hang out much throughout my final week. I was helping Bea and Julie pack; I was at work; I had to go home and Skype my mum. The last time I saw him that summer, I felt as if our whole romance had been a bit of a lie. We kissed one another and we had a hug and he asked if I wanted to come back to his apartment, for old times' sake, and I said no – I had to help Bea and Julie (I didn't).

I did, at that stage, have his Italian mobile number – we would exchange curt, badly spelled text messages in a mélange of European languages, usually to arrange where or when to meet – but, when I left, our communications ceased. I tried to look him up on Facebook once or twice, but I didn't know his real name, and 'Poncho' brought up thousands of Mexican boys, none of whom looked familiar.

We saw one another again once, after that. A year later, coming up to my end-of-year exams, I went to Milan to stay with Andrew and Achille, friends of Bea's I'd got to know while I was there. The idea was to bone up on my Italian before my oral exam, but really I spent most of my time reading (in English) and eating pastries (in silence).

It took me until my last night there to muster up the courage to go to Cape Town, to say hi to Sergio and Silvia and to take a look into the bar next door, on the off chance that Poncho would be there. He was waiting tables outside when I arrived, squinting in the sunlight. He smiled, placed his tray on a table and walked over to me, embraced me. 'You're back!' he said.

I was embarrassed by his effusiveness and he could tell. He backed off, picked his tray back up, glanced inside at his boss, an elderly woman who always seemed to frown upon any displays of happiness or enthusiasm by her staff. 'How long you are here for?' he asked me; I told him I was leaving the next day. 'Can you come back? Tonight? I finish at one,' he told me, taking another look inside, shuffling chairs into position, trying to look busy. I told him I would.

I went back to Andrew and Achilles' for the evening. We ate oversized pasta shells with green peas and bacon pieces and I told them about seeing Poncho. 'He looked just the same!' I told them. I did not say that I had arranged to meet him later.

I don't know why, but I didn't meet him that night. Something about it felt pointless. I was tired. I was flying back the following morning. It wasn't like anything could come of it. I didn't have his number any more, so I couldn't even tell him I wasn't coming. I went to bed before midnight, tossing and turning in the late-spring humidity, feeling bad, but not bad enough to get up, not bad enough to follow through with what I'd promised.

I never saw Poncho again. Every couple of months, I'd think about him and try searching for variations of his nickname on Facebook. When Google Street View launched, I would put in the address of the bar he worked at, peering through the windows to see if he was there, cleaning tables or taking orders. He never was.

One day, not that long ago, I went on and checked out the street where he worked but found that the bar had shut down. Its signage was gone, replaced now with shabby graffiti and a torn piece of awning, hanging, at an angle, from one side of the building.

Adam

Upon returning from my summer in Milan, I was – once again – not sure if college was for me. I had six weeks to decide, so I took a job at Brown Thomas, a luxury department store in Dublin city centre, imagining this might be my gateway into a job in fashion buying. I loved the idea of being responsible for the clothing selection in shops, distilling the catwalk trends down to their composite parts, ripe for consumers to pick and choose their must-haves.

It didn't occur to me at the time, but the fact that every single sales season, I would see, discounted by up to 70 per cent, the very items I had bought earlier that year at full price, was perhaps a sign that I was not always drawn to the items that were sure to sell. On the contrary, I was convinced that I had a great eye for predicting what was sure to be popular, and what wasn't.

I was assigned to the designer floor, giving advice to women shopping for €500 day dresses. I helped an affluent eighteen-year-old and her mother choose the best of three €1,000 evening gowns to wear to her school's debs; later, I would see her in *Image* magazine's debutante special, resplendent in Julien Macdonald and with a perfect sheen of high-end makeup, a spotty-faced boy on her arm wearing an ill-fitting tux.

We worked on commission, so it paid to pander to wealthier customers and I was very good at it. I knew how to walk the line between honesty and tact, never shying away from telling someone when a dress was too small. In any case, you could tell from their faces in the fitting-room mirrors who was loving what; I would never have discouraged someone from parting with their hard-earned cash if I could see that they had truly fallen in love with that season's must-have sequined shift.

I was there four weeks when I copped that, yet again, this wasn't the job for me. I adored fashion, and I loved working in a customer-facing role, getting to chat to people all day long, but I hated being told what to do and the tendency – in my experience – of managers to disregard the opinions of their subordinates, whether or not said opinions contained any merit.

The death knell came when my manager chastised me for 'ignoring' a woman who was browsing the Diane von Furstenberg collection. When she had walked into my area, I had smiled at her and said hello – she had averted her eyes. Like I said, you had to be able to read the room. Still, I was instructed to walk over and ask if she was okay. As predicted, she muttered a yes and high-tailed it to the exit. (I told you so.)

There is a weird impulse in our society, I think, to praise young people who know what they want to do after university – but we don't place enough emphasis on enjoying the experience of being there, regardless of whether or not our chosen degree will lead to a lucrative career. I have since discovered capitalism's inexorable truth: working is a scam and the scam is structural. Put it off for as long as possible.

By the time I went back to university, I'd missed the first two weeks of lectures, which was not a big deal – they had mostly been taken up with introductions and course outlines, and I could catch up from my classmates. The bigger problem was that I had nowhere to live; all of the on-campus accommodation was full, and the friends I had made in my first year had already found their housemates.

I stayed with Donna and Antoinette, two English sisters I'd met the year previously, for a few weeks, sleeping on their sofa and, on the weekends they went to visit their Irish parents in Mayo, in one or other of their beds, being careful to change the sheets and leave nothing disturbed. They'd given me their permission, but still, it felt like the polite thing to do.

I eventually found a room in a shared house with three friends from the midlands. They'd had someone for the fourth bedroom, but she had decided to drop out and now they needed to fill the space. My room was massive, with a king-sized bed and enormous wardrobe, luxuries rarely seen in student accommodation.

I wondered why one of them hadn't taken

this – the best – room until I realised that I was paying about €100 per month more than anyone else for the privilege. My parents were covering my rent and it was within their budget, just about, so I hadn't questioned it at first and, when I did find out, decided not to kick up a fuss (or to tell my mum and dad).

I had joined the choir the previous year, having met the conductor at an audition for the university musical society. I'd been offered a part in the chorus but, having taken offence at this insult (I saw myself as a supporting actor, if not the lead, despite having quite bad stage fright and a tendency to get pitchy in front of an audience), never went back to the musical society. When he approached me to sing in the choir, telling me I had a 'beautiful' voice, it seemed rude to say no.

As it happens, choir was a godsend – and quite possibly the thing that kept me tethered to university until graduation. I've never quite felt like I had a 'tribe', being neither sporty nor swotty, not quite sociable enough to make the type of friends you'd go out with every Friday night, and never studious enough to hang out with the quiet crowd in the library, many of whom would end up becoming lawyers or teachers.

We rehearsed twice a week and performed weekly, as well as taking trips to choral competitions in Ireland and, once, to Italy, where we spent five glorious days by Lake Garda, singing an incredible composition by Eric Whitacre, which, even now, I sometimes play to remind myself of that time.

Adam was a bass in the choir, in situ well before I joined. He was a year ahead of me in university, studying engineering, which always seemed, somehow, like too solid a subject choice for him. He played the guitar and loved cooking and gardening; I felt like he would've been better suited to something more ethereal, less pragmatic.

He never said this to me, but I think he looked down on people who did arts degrees. I didn't feel like he came from the kind of family that would have approved of spending three years doing something with no solid end goal.

His father, now retired, had worked for a while as a truck driver, moving freight from one side of America to the other. 'He'd just always wanted to do it,' Adam told me. That was his dad's dream. Later, when he retired, he would get into acting, performing in a selection of plays around the country, but that was not the type of thing he could ever have considered for 'work'.

Adam was tall, with long, curly hair. Occasionally, he would tie it back in a bun – most memorably, for the day he got his passport photographs taken. 'If I cut my hair in the future, I want to be recognisable,' he told me. See? Pragmatic.

I'm not quite sure when, or even why, I decided that he was going to be the man for me – I mean, within the choral society there were slim pickings, so in that context at least he made sense – but once I had decided, I approached the project with a determination I have never quite managed to apply to anything else, like work or school. Somehow, securing a boyfriend always seems, in the moment, more important than anything else.

Adam had recently kissed another girl from choir on a night out, I learned through the gossip grapevine, and I began to obsess over the differences between us. She struck me as the type of girl who would sleep in her eyeliner and wake up looking cool; her hair had that kind of unwashed look to it that was very covetable in the early noughties, when Alexa Chung's claim that she didn't own a hairbrush impressed us all.

I was never quite convinced that he wouldn't have, ultimately, preferred to be with her – but she was the kind of free spirit who didn't want a relationship. 'I'm too young!' she told me once, as we drank warm wine out of plexiglass tumblers in the bedroom of some hostel we were staying in the night before a performance.

What must it be like, I wondered, *not* to want to be in a relationship? I could only be happy with the addition of another person, I thought, while these people were happy on their own – they had achieved true relationship neutrality. I was envious while also being quietly critical, as if I was watching a documentary about polyamory, pretending it was cool and fine 'if that's what people want to do!' while really thinking, *That's a weird thing to want.*

Ours was a kind of textbook romance, in the sense that we went on a date before we'd even kissed – a rarity in those days of drunken snogs followed by days of wishing you'd hear from them followed by another drunken snog – although it was undoubtedly helped along by the meddling of a mutual friend, who I tasked with sending him an 'accidental' text, just, you know, to help things on their way.

She and I spent hours debating the content of said text; the idea that it had been sent in error needed to be somewhat believable, and it was also essential that he wouldn't know exactly who it was about, in order to open up a line of conversation. We quipped about leading horses to water, then finally agreed on 'I can't believe you fancy Adam! Since when?!'

I don't think he ever did find out about this little matchmaking game – he wrote back immediately to tell her that she'd sent the text to the wrong person, and demanded to know who it was meant for. When she told him it was me, he went quiet for a few days – you can imagine the high-stress conversations my friend and I were having about him – then texted me to ask if I'd like to go to the cinema with him.

He bought the tickets ahead of time, refusing to hear of me paying for them – then he insisted on forking out for the snacks, too. This kind of chivalry was relatively new to me. I mean, I'd gone out with nice guys before, but no one who'd seriously argued with me when I offered to go halves.

I can't remember what the movie was, only that it was fine – and that, afterwards, we sat in silence next to one another as the rest of the audience members filed out in twos. Just as the theatre emptied completely and I thought we might turn to one another and kiss – we had been brushing arms throughout the movie, 'accidentally' touching one another pretty regularly – the lights came up and the ushers bustled in, sweeping and vacuuming loudly. We didn't say anything, getting out of our seats almost in unison and with great haste.

Taxis were an expense only to be incurred when absolutely necessary, so he walked me home and, outside the door of the house I shared with the three girls I barely knew, he leaned down – he was over six foot to my five foot six – and kissed me.

I could feel his left canine, which was at a slight angle to the rest of his teeth, as I slipped my tongue between his lips. It became one of my favourite things about him, this slight imperfection that he never mentioned. It didn't seem to bother him – either that or he'd never even thought about it, which added to the attraction.

I didn't invite him in, because – and this was how romance worked in my twentysomething brain – I thought I could genuinely quite like him. I didn't want to waste the attraction between us on one night, or even a handful of nights, together. I wanted him to put me in the 'serious' category, not in the 'casual' category. I was building up to something here, something that felt important and meaningful, something that would make me important, give me meaning, in turn.

He would text me later that night to say he had a nice time. To thank me. It was a short text, but I was over the moon, and determined, for perhaps the first time in my life, to play it cool.

It shouldn't surprise you – it did not surprise me – to learn that I did not, in fact, play it cool. From that very first date, that very first kiss outside the front porch of the three-bedroom semi-detached house I shared in a housing estate in Galway, I was smitten. Much to my surprise and delight, though, so was he.

He was a virgin, which did not feel like a big deal to me, although he was determined to wait until he felt 'ready', which, at the time, felt like a very girls' magazine approach to sex. On one of the first evenings we spent alone together, he came over to my house to watch a movie. (The girls were out somewhere, avid fans of student nights where they could pre-drink at home and share the cost of a taxi to the club by rowing in together, frequently coordinating outfits and eyeshadows before leaving the house.)

We were lying on the couch, kissing one another softly, when I asked if he wanted to play 'anywhere but here', a game whose playing seemed entirely designed to reinforce the ego of the asker. I would ask him, 'If you could be anywhere in the world, with anyone, where would you be and with whom?' and I would hope that he'd refuse to answer, say that he wouldn't be anywhere but here, that he wouldn't be with anyone but me. At the very least, I held out hope that he would take me with him to a paradise island, to his favourite holiday destination, to a city he'd always wanted to visit.

He thought for a while – too long, honestly – and

then told me he'd like to go back home, to his parents' house, to the time before his mum had left his dad, when all three of them were together, an unbroken unit.

I was taken aback. It's not that I hadn't thought of men as complex creatures with a full set of emotional wants and needs, but perhaps that I hadn't quite experienced them as such. At least not any with whom I'd been romantically involved, at least not at an intimate moment where I had opened a door expecting to be greeted with a compliment, and instead found myself stepping through and into the labyrinthine depths of his past.

From then on, I started to see Adam differently – as if the flat outline I had of him in my mind, on to which I projected all of my hopes for him, but mostly for myself, had suddenly expanded. He had harsh edges; his layers were uncovered. I began to be more careful with him and his feelings, and to feel more protective of him. In a way, I think it was then that I started to care about him more fully as a person in his own right, rather than just a vector through which I could perform my own romantic destiny.

We were an official couple within a month, and we remained so for over three years, after he graduated from college and got a job at an engineering firm in Galway, through to my graduation and commencement of a master's degree in Dublin. I started my MA in an economic boom time, but within the year we were deep into the recession of 2007. All of a sudden, putting time and money into a master's seemed like a foolish misstep – in journalism, of all things! Didn't I know newspapers were dying? (I did.)

I remember, vividly, snippets of our relationship, like flashes in a rom-com montage designed to indicate the passing of time. We went to Amsterdam on holiday to visit my cousin Philip, who was then living there. He met us at the train station with bikes, and wheeled our cases home himself. Adam, of course, gamely hopped straight up on the bike Philip had brought; I was horrified at the thought that I'd have to pedal myself home, even more so when I realised that the bike had coaster brakes, activated by pushing backwards on the pedals, which I'd never used before.

Amsterdam is quite possibly the worst place in the world to topple off a bike, let me tell you – and I have toppled off a bike in quite a few places. (The second worst is on the tram tracks in Dublin city centre, right outside the gates of Trinity College, thronged, at all times, with tourists and students who think they're smarter than you.)

We visited the Anne Frank House and cycled our bikes along the canals and ate Indonesian food in a restaurant I have thought of at least once a month ever since. We ordered a coconut beef curry that tasted like nothing I had ever had before, nor since. (No, I can't remember the name.)

Back in Ireland, we spent weekends at his dad's place in the country with his dog, who was an excellent swimmer, and his dad, who was an excellent cook. His mum was living in Dublin, and we visited her too, but never stayed. She lived in a small, one-bedroom apartment ten minutes from Phoenix Park and did not have a dog.

After I'd started my master's, in late 2007, Adam moved to Dublin – ostensibly to be with me, but also to branch out and get some experience, in terms of both work and life, outside of the West. We both decided that it would be good for him to meet new people, to forge a life that wasn't entirely tied up with mine, so he moved into a house in an affluent suburb with three young professional men he didn't know.

I was living with my parents at the time and couldn't have afforded to pay rent, so the question of living together never came up in any serious way. By the start of the following year, however, I was working part-time at the *Irish Times* while I completed my thesis, and probably earning as much, for two days' work, as he was at his full-time, entry-level engineering job. Still, we thought, it made more sense for me to stay at home and for him to live with 'the lads' in his new house.

He joined a local football club – as a way to make friends, but also because he had played down home, and loved the sport – and signed himself up for tennis with one of his work colleagues. We mostly saw one another on weekends, when I would stay at his place and we would wander out for brunch on Sunday mornings like the young suburban couple I wanted us to become.

Within six months of commencing this new life – the football, the tennis, the job – Adam was let go.

With the downturn in economic growth, builders were going bust left, right and centre and structural engineers were not in great demand. Adam found someone to take over his lease and went back to his old job in Galway, grateful that he'd left on good terms and things were not (yet) quite so dire outside of the capital.

The economy had crashed quickly, and spectacularly, and it wasn't long before what seemed like dozens of our peers had begun to leave the country, some for the US but most for Australia and New Zealand, where the economic missteps of the likes of Lehman Brothers weren't making quite as much of an impact.

Adam heard tales of plentiful jobs in engineering Down Under; such-and-such a friend was there just two weeks when he had a great job and an apartment with a view of Sydney Opera House. He wanted to go, and we began to discuss the possibility of us both applying for a visa and heading to Perth, or to Melbourne, for a year or two – I liked the idea of a city *other* than Sydney, which to me always felt like a larger version of Gran Canaria, full of drunk Irish people and karaoke bars.

I had never really entertained the idea of moving abroad before. I studied Italian in my undergraduate degree, and the course was designed to include a year on Erasmus in Italy, but I had decided not to do the Erasmus year, citing my age – I had taken a year out after school and already felt as though I was behind a lot of my friends – and the fact that I had already spent a summer in Italy and had a good grasp of the language. Of course, it was really because I was going out with Adam, and I couldn't imagine myself going to live in a different country without him.

This was not, as it turns out, something that would stop him, even three years into our relationship. I began to have second thoughts, worried that I would be giving up my dream job at the *Irish Times*, a place I'd always dreamed of working, to clear tables at some grotty Australian restaurant while I searched for the needle in the haystack: a job in journalism.

Ultimately, he decided to go, and I decided to stay, and we both decided that our relationship was not a good candidate for an even-longer-distance run.

We'd found the Galway–Dublin relationship commute difficult enough; I'd plan the 'perfect' weekend we could spend together after two weeks apart, and then something would happen – a small argument, or even a tense word – and I'd feel like the whole weekend was ruined.

I found that it wasn't being apart that was difficult, per se; rather, it was being together and struggling not to see that moment of togetherness as some kind of microcosm of the relationship writ large. A bad weekend could mean that our entire relationship was doomed; we would spend the following weeks trying to come back from the disappointment of it all.

We broke up on the phone – a sad discussion that ended in a mutual decision that felt right, but also terrible and heartbreaking.

I would see Adam once more, on the rooftop of a

shopping centre in Dublin, where we had met for a final, devastating coffee, and where he would hand me a shoebox full of my things – tampons and a toothbrush and two T-shirts I'd left in his house – and say, 'Well! Have a good life!' in a cheery, awkward way that made me want to shrivel up and die.

We would email back and forward a little over the ensuing years, most recently when I started to write this book and emailed to give him some warning. 'I'm feeling famous already!' he said.

I feel sad when I think about our relationship, but also glad that we met, that I orchestrated that 'accidental' text, that he asked me on that first cinema date. He was, I think, the first man I properly loved. I got to know him as a whole person, not just as 'my boyfriend'; he existed before me and he existed after me and, even when we were together, he existed without me, too. I could probably take some tips from him.

Dan

My sister never liked Dan. I think, actually, she disliked him before she met him, based on the fact that she thought I should be taking some time off dating, time to actively be single, instead of my usual status of 'single-but-frantically-looking'.

But she disliked him when she met him, too. He was three years older than her, about five inches shorter and desperately insecure about both his height and his perceived lack of 'success' in life, whatever that means. She made some light-hearted joke about him that he didn't appreciate; he told her she came across as 'arrogant', then laughed as if he, too, was joking.

When we met he was thirty-five, unemployed and back living with his parents in rural Ireland. His two children, who were four and two at the time, lived in the UK with their British mother.

We had met online, on one of those pre-dating-app websites that allowed you to message whoever you liked the look of. He had dark hair and eyes, and a deep tan; in one photograph, he wore a tight khaki

T-shirt. He looked like he might be in the army, but his bio said he was an engineer. I'd had great luck with engineers, I thought.

We messaged back and forth a lot before we eventually met for a drink in the Metropole Bar on Dublin's Dame Street. He didn't tell me this at the time, but he'd been at a singles' event on Harcourt Street the night before and tacked me on to his trip, I suppose killing two birds with one stone.

We had told one another all about our dating history, our likes and dislikes, our families and what, exactly, we were looking for. 'Nothing serious,' I had said, and for a time believed it, not quite realising at the time that the phrase 'nothing serious' is like catnip for straight men.

Dan told me about his children – a boy and a girl, who lived with his ex in the UK. They had been on the cusp of breaking up when she became pregnant with their second child, he said, and had broken up before he was born. He tried to visit them once a month, if finances allowed; he refused to fly Ryanair, 'on principle', he said, whatever that meant, so his flights between Dublin and the UK were notoriously pricey.

Our first date was one of those never-ending, where-did-the-time-go dates. We had met in the afternoon, which always feels like a good idea for a first date; it's easier to get out of, citing dinner plans, or family engagements, than 8 p.m. drinks, after which time, what can you *really* be doing? We went from one bar to another, stopping midway for drinks, ending up at a late bar until 2 a.m., when, finally, we agreed that it was home time.

I had planned to stay at a relative's house a fifteen-minute walk from the city centre; they were away, so I had the place to myself, and by some coincidence he was staying in a Travelodge just around the corner, so we walked back together.

When we got to my door, I invited him in for a cup of tea – the classic Irish come-on – and he agreed, so we stood in the kitchen sipping tea and chatting awkwardly for another hour before he said he'd have to go, and I walked him back out to the street, all the while wondering what the hell was going on.

All of the signs were there! We'd spent more than eight hours together! He'd definitely been touching my arm at one stage! He told me that I was much prettier than I'd looked in my photos! (Mind you, I've never been sure whether or not this is a compliment.) And now he was just ... going to walk away, without so much as a backward glance?

I was standing in the doorway as we said goodbye, a small step up from him – which, in hindsight, must have struck him as cruel – when I decided to take the bull by the horns or, rather, the man by the shirt lapels, and kiss him, probably rather roughly. (The idea of asking someone if they wanted to be kissed had never once occurred to me; it always seemed better to just go for it, especially if you were standing next to a door you could slam if and when you were rebuffed.)

To my great relief, he kissed me back, and then we

retraced our steps, back into the house and up, now, to the bedroom I was staying in, which had once been my cousin Abigail's childhood bedroom. The mantelpiece in the bedroom of this old Georgian three-storey – fireplaces in every room – still boasted the detritus of her teenage years: concert tickets and half-burned candles and a plait of her once waist-length hair that she had cut off, all at once, à la Jo March (albeit not to sell, but to keep).

We didn't have sex that night – 'I actually like you,' he told me, again setting out his stall, declaring pretty early on that I was in the 'serious' rather than 'casual' category and, as such, we couldn't have sex just yet – and he snuck off back to his lodgings in the early hours of the morning.

I slept for maybe ninety minutes and went to work, exhausted and headachey but thrilled with how well the date had gone, and buoyed by the prospect of this burgeoning romance.

When I called my sister – she was living in Paris then, having moved from Milan to work at an edgy French fashion house – to tell her about our date, she had a distinct air of 'I told you so' about her. 'So, you have a new boyfriend, then,' she said. I could hear her rolling her eyes.

'No!' I protested. 'But he's *really* nice.'

Was he really nice? I ask myself this a lot, about a lot of people – okay, a lot of *men* – I once thought were 'really nice'. What does 'really nice' even mean? If someone described *me* as 'really nice', I think I'd be slightly insulted. It feels like an insipid, non-specific description, like calling someone 'harmless' or, the worst one of all, saying that their 'heart is in the right place'.

He wasn't particularly funny. Nor was he especially generous, although I'm not sure whether or not he would have been in different circumstances.

I was, by then, working between three and five days a week at the *Irish Times* on a freelance contract, which meant that I was on quite a substantial per diem rate, which included an allowance for magazines that often amounted to €200 or so each month, apparently for 'research'.

To be fair, at that time I was spending well over €200 each month on glossy women's magazines, but my research was more focused on how to lose weight, achieve bouncier, shinier curls or play hard to get than it was on production values, design principles or headline-writing tricks.

As a result of my relative affluence, I paid for most of our dates, something that he suffered loudly.

'I can't *believe* how much you get paid for the work you do!' he would announce at regular intervals, while I thought, *He's right.* The fact that the work was easy *because I was good at it* did not occur to either of us at the time. I suspect it hasn't occurred to him since, either.

The first time we had sex, I didn't come. If you are a straight, cisgender, heterosexual woman reading this, that fact will quite probably *not* be surprising to you; it wasn't until I was well into my twenties that I started to wonder why, exactly, sex seems to begin and end with a man's boner and orgasm, respectively. Where do my physical cues come into it?

In any case, Dan made it clear, pretty early on, that I had some kind of shortfall that was inhibiting my orgasm. 'Did you come?' he would ask, and then say things like, 'It's so weird ... my ex used to come all the time in that position.' By 'that position' – again, cishet women, prepare *not* to be surprised – he meant 'missionary'.

I was, of course, embarrassed by this – if you'll excuse the pun – shortcoming of mine. When I told him that I'd had more luck achieving orgasm through oral sex, he told me, 'Oh, I don't do that – it's just something I've never enjoyed.' We dated for a year, and he never once asked if there was anything he could do to facilitate my orgasm; similarly, after that early, gentle suggestion, I never spoke up about it.

Needless to say, blow jobs were 'just something' he definitely enjoyed – my orgasm was my problem, and he very rarely mentioned it again. When he did, it was to wonder at what exactly the problem with my body was. So weird!

A few months into our relationship, I moved into a house share halfway between my parents' house and my office in Dublin. It was time for me to move out, I announced, but the true driving factor was my desire to show Dan how grown-up I was.

I find it hard to put this in writing, but he frequently pointed out how odd and immature it was that I was living at home – while he, nine years my senior, *also lived at home*. He acted as though his living situation was an accident, while mine was an odd choice that said something terrible and damning about my personality.

When his sister and brother-in-law decided to build a house and he moved in with them to work as their on-site engineer, he acted as though he had got a job in the City of London and was living in the penthouse apartment of the Shard – despite the fact that he was sleeping in their guest room and spent all seven nights of the week nursing a pint in the local pub.

The pints galled me slightly, but I was – and am still – always a bit reticent to say things that could be categorised as 'nagging'. Pointing out that he could never afford to pay for dinner but could afford to go to the pub every night definitely fell into that category.

Similarly, when, six months into our relationship, he took up a new hobby, I felt as though it would be unfair of me to point out that his money could be better spent flying to see his children more frequently, occasionally forking out for date night or even saving to move into a place that didn't belong to one of his family members.

The hobby in question? Sky-diving. He took up sky-diving.

If there was a list of the world's most expensive – and frankly ridiculous – hobbies, I think sky-diving would surely be in the top five. (I think this based solely on my own recollections of his sky-diving days and no concrete facts whatsoever.)

Sky-diving became the thing – instead of me – that

occupied him each and every weekend, and more than once he would cancel a planned weekend with me in Dublin because the conditions were 'ideal' for a jump.

'You don't mind, do you?' he'd ask. 'You know I don't have any other real hobbies.'

It was true, he didn't. But hobbies, to my mind, were reading or going for walks, not spending hours in a flight suit learning to fall out of a plane in a specific, 'right' way.

Still, far be it from me . . .

For our first Christmas together, I bought him the gift of a trip to Paris, to coincide with the date of my birthday in February. He'd never been, and I wanted him to experience the City of Love with me. I found us a hotel near the Marais but also, unbeknownst to me, in the heart of the tourist district, right above a pizza restaurant and across the road from an Irish pub. He bought me a book and a bottle of perfume I'd really wanted.

In hindsight, I think he was humiliated by the disparity between our gifts. I have never been someone who cares about the price of things, and I loved the gifts he'd given me. I knew that he didn't have a huge amount of disposable income – at least, he didn't have a huge amount that wasn't going on sky-diving lessons – and I hadn't expected him to buy me something of 'equal' monetary value.

But his resentment was growing, and by the time we boarded the flight to Paris – Ryanair, which I'm sure he was absolutely enraged by, but I wasn't a millionaire – I was very clearly irritating him greatly.

Dan

Everything was wrong. The hotel was shitty (it was), the area was overpriced (also true), the weather was rubbish (unfortunately I had to agree). We wandered around the city aimlessly, but without the devil-may-care sense of whimsy I had imagined we would have when I thought of our romantic weekend in Paris.

In one particularly bizarre moment, he grew incredibly agitated with me because I suggested we cross the road to the left, instead of going across and *then* to the left. He grabbed my hand and pulled me in the direction he had chosen.

'Why do you have to argue about *everything*?!' he exclaimed, and I realised that he really didn't like to feel as if he wasn't in charge. I began to pity him; this weekend that I had planned must have stung.

Sunday was my birthday, and I spent the day waiting for him to reveal the birthday surprise he had surely planned for me. A gift, at the very least, but I was also expecting a nice restaurant to have been booked, maybe paid for with money he had been diverting from his sky-diving fund for this very purpose.

In the afternoon, Dan announced that he wanted to watch the rugby – Ireland was playing a little later, while England was playing first. Forgive me if I do not remember who they were up against.

Though I had known him to watch a game of rugby if it happened to be on the television while he was in the room, or if he happened to be in the pub on game night, he had never before expressed any real interest in the sport.

I am old enough and wise enough now to know a bit better, but I will confess that I believed this might be an elaborate ruse, and that I would agree to go and watch the rugby and find myself IN MY BIRTHDAY SURPRISE! This may not be as much of a spoiler for you as it would have been for me back then, but rest assured: there was no birthday surprise.

Anyway, off we went to watch the rugby, in the dingy Irish pub across the road from our dingy hotel. I had a vodka and Diet Coke; he had a pint, then another, then another. By the time Ireland had been beaten he was slightly tipsy and seemed to be in relatively jovial form. I made a joke about him slurring his words; he laughed and told me, affectionately, to pipe down.

When we left the pub it was dark and I was starving. *This is it*, I thought. *My birthday surprise is coming up.*

'Where will we go for dinner?' I asked, coyly.

'Let's just get pizza over there,' he suggested, pointing to the dingy pizza restaurant beneath our dingy hotel.

I truly wish that, at that very moment, I had thrown the mother of all hissy fits. I wish that I had called him selfish and thoughtless and cried and screamed in the middle of the street, causing a scene that would have been his worst nightmare.

Instead, I walked hand in hand with him into the pizza restaurant and sat across from him as we ate our pizza, each bite harder and harder to gulp down past the growing lump in my throat.

At one stage, Dan grew very silent, which was

always a bad omen. I asked him what was wrong. He said nothing. I continued to eat my pizza. We didn't speak for a good ten minutes. I asked him again – and again. After the third or fourth time, he finally spat it out: 'You just think you're right about everything all the time!' he said.

I had no idea where this was coming from. Although, I will caveat this by saying: it's true. I do think I'm right about everything – honestly, who doesn't? Why would anyone say anything if they *didn't* think they were right? – but I wasn't quite sure which interaction in particular had elicited this outburst. I could feel myself getting hot and red-faced with anger and upset and humiliation. (This was not, I should say, a very good birthday surprise.)

'What are you talking about?' I asked him.

'You're so fucking high and mighty,' he said then, making it clear that he had some things he wished to get off his chest, and get them off his chest he would, right here and now.

'Back there in the pub, slagging the way I was talking – who do you think you are?'

I could feel myself beginning to cry, both because of what he was saying to me and because of the unfairness of it all. I had taken him away for this lovely weekend, we had spent the entire day – my birthday! – doing what he wanted to do and now he was subjecting me to a character assassination that had come out of nowhere and seemingly needed to be executed in public.

I stood up, pushed my chair back and went to

walk out of the restaurant. It was only when I got to the door that I remembered that he had no money. I walked back to our waiter, now standing, baffled, by the kitchen, with the crème brûlée I had ordered in hand.

'*Non*,' I told him. '*Non. Je veux payer.*' No. I want to pay.

He didn't charge for the dessert.

We went back to our hotel room, silently packed our cases and – still silently, we didn't speak for the rest of the evening – got into bed. Halfway through the night he snaked a hand around my waist and kissed me on the shoulder. 'Are we okay?' he asked and I, like a coward, said, 'Yes,' deciding that there was no point in breaking up now, in Paris, when we had a long trip to the airport and flight home to get through. No, I would do it later, at a better time.

We both did a good job of acting like everything was fine. We had croissants and coffee in the café on the corner, then went to get the bus out to Ryanair's idea of a 'Paris' airport, an hour outside the city.

It wasn't until we got to the security line that his rage once again began to spill over. His bag was chosen for a random inspection and, as they produced a camera I had never seen before in our year of dating – and which had certainly not been taken out *once* in Paris, this city he had never before visited – I asked, 'Where did you get *that*?!'

He reacted as if I'd pointed at him and said, 'This man is a terrorist, sir!', turning towards me and spitting, 'For *fuck's* sake, Rosemary, what the *fuck* is wrong with you?! It's a *fucking* camera!' Everyone looked at us. I remember trying to bite down my tears as I tied the laces on my shoes.

We didn't say a word until we got to Dublin, although he rested his head on my shoulder through-out the flight, falling into a deep sleep that gave me a strong desire to pour my hot coffee on to his lap.

When we got to the arrivals hall in Dublin Airport, he looked at me and said, 'I think I'll just head home, all right?' We had planned to meet my parents for a birthday brunch, and to regale them with tales of our weekend in *la belle Paris*.

'I think that's for the best,' I agreed.

'I'll call you later?' he asked, leaning in to kiss my cheek. I think I laughed, ever so slightly – why would he be calling me later?

'Don't bother,' I said. 'I think we both know this is over.'

Apparently only one of us knew this was over – Dan thought that we'd had a fight, one we could recover from once we'd had a few days apart. He suggested that I take the week to think it over (although it was very clear that what he meant was, 'take the week to calm down'); he would call me the following weekend.

I told him that he could call me the next weekend if he really wanted to, but that it was over. He looked sceptical, gave me his 'sure, Jan' face.

A few days later, as promised, he did call me – and was once again incredulous at the fact that I was tell-ing him it was over.

'You treated me terribly,' I told him.

'It was just a fight,' he said.

But it wasn't just a fight, was it? It was the culmination of months of simmering resentment at his younger girlfriend and her frankly ridiculous salary, her ability to swan around doing whatever she liked and reluctance to be told which traffic lights to cross the road at.

We met one more time a few weeks later, at an Italian restaurant in Dundrum, so that he could return the carry-on suitcase he'd borrowed for that fateful French weekend, a suitcase that belonged to my mother and that she simply would not write off as a casualty of my romantic dalliances.

'I've really missed you,' he told me, over pasta and dough sticks.

'Mmm-hmm,' I said. 'Mmm-hmm.'

I was absolutely determined to stick to my guns, to stay broken up, and not to get sucked in by the flattery of knowing that he regretted our breakup. The truth was, I hated being single and I missed being someone's girlfriend, but I knew that I deserved better than this man who seemed to resent my success and saw it only as a reflection of his failure.

We never saw one another again although, true to form, I occasionally look him up and, because we live in a hellscape where everyone's lives are online to some degree, I know that he is married with a small baby and a beautiful wife who is one of the most stylish women I've ever seen. I hope he's given up the sky-diving.

Gary

I have never considered myself an early adopter – of anything, really. When it comes to fashion trends, more specifically, I tend to spend the first few weeks of any viral trend mocking it relentlessly until I cave, spectacularly, buying the most expensive version of each given item and saying things like, 'Well, I just like this iteration – not *all* of them.'

In terms of Twitter, though, I probably was an early adopter. I was on Twitter in the days when nobody was really on Twitter or, if they were, their only contributions were their weekly star signs, auto-tweeted from a site they forgot they'd signed up to. They probably didn't remember their passwords any more, couldn't be bothered trying to log on to undo the horoscope stuff. It didn't matter – no one was really on Twitter anyway.

I was a regular tweeter when it was fresh and new and you could have all-day conversations with the same group of twenty or thirty people, all of whom were also early adopters to this newfangled form of social media, one none of us could really see lasting.

Where was its business model? How would it make money? We couldn't imagine it.

Instead, Twitter became a club of sorts, where we would share anecdotes from our respective days, give restaurant recommendations or offer old furniture to one another. I gave away my Nintendo Wii on Twitter. (Surely the joy of a games console is that you get to sit still, to be sedentary. The Nintendo Wii turned that on its head, and that's before we've even got to the vast insults levelled at me by the Wii Fit, which gave me an avatar that looked like a very short, rotund man in his forties.)

The early group of us on Twitter were known – perhaps only among ourselves – as the Twitterati. We all knew one another in that incestuous kind of way that people know each other in Ireland. Even if we hadn't met in real life, we knew someone who knew the other someone, which alleviated any sense of stranger danger that we might otherwise have had about these people we now conversed with on a daily basis.

It was fun to be a part of something that was in its infancy. It was a warm, inclusive feeling; in the very early days, we would get invited to events purely because we were active 'tweeters'. I spent one St Patrick's Day in the Guinness factory drinking all I could drink (which was not a lot, I'll confess) simply because Guinness was hoping that I might tweet something effusive using the #homeofguinness hashtag. I was happy to oblige.

It was fun, too, to watch relationships being made

and destroyed. People who were, one week, the best of friends, trading insights into their favourite films and arranging to watch TV together (at least virtually, so that they could discuss the goings-on in real time) would fall out over what seemed like the smallest of slights. But if you were really paying attention, you would have seen the cracks begin to form – you could mark, as if on a map, the route they took that veered away from one another, rather than bringing them closer together.

It took longer to get to know people on Twitter than it did in real life, and sometimes you didn't get the full picture until you were Twitter besties. The breakups were a wrench.

I met Gary on Twitter. He was the kind of rabble-rousing devil's advocate I found oddly irresistible. Though I found many of his views repulsive – that Irish women who found themselves with unwanted pregnancies should be locked up until they give birth, for example (at that time abortion was still illegal in Ireland, and so this was a popular discussion topic) – he argued them with an intelligence I found bizarrely attractive.

I think I was, for a time, able to convince myself that an individual's views were not necessarily reflective of their personality – at least not entirely. In later years, and especially the years I've spent living in the US, I've come to feel that these things are, in fact, black and white. I can't imagine flirting with a staunch Republican, for example, or entertaining the possibility of romance with an opponent of abortion rights. But the past truly is a foreign country.

Others in the Twitter clique noticed our mutual attraction before, I think, we did. I had very little clue what he looked like; his avatar was a blurry photograph of him taken at a wedding, and from a distance. Ten years later, it was unlikely that this bore more than a passing resemblance to modern-day Gary.

We argued with one another a lot, but always with a wink – albeit not in emoji form. Those would come later. I have always taken great pleasure in a heated discussion (although not, I would like to stress, an argument) and in Gary I found a willing opponent. He seemed to always be there, ready and waiting with a witty riposte to whatever mundanity I had chosen to share with my followers.

Our flirtation continued for weeks before either of us was brave enough to suggest bringing it into the real world. In a way, I wish we had continued like that; I found debating with him fun, and I was flattered by the attention he paid me in an ever-increasing sea of voices. In a way, I think taking our romance offline sounded the death knell – I have since learned, over years of online dating, that the more you build the romance up before that first meeting, the more disappointing that moment is sure to be. There are no perfect men (as, I'm sure, there are no perfect women).

I don't have the messages we exchanged in private any more, but I remember them being similarly fun. They did, of course, grow increasingly risqué, until he invited me over to his place for dinner. He offered to cook me steak, which is, I think, the straight man's idea of food foreplay. When he asked how I liked mine, I told him I liked it rare – which is true, but was also, weirdly, a great source of pride for me at the time. I knew that a woman who likes her steak rare is a man's woman.

I knew, too, the minute he greeted me in the lobby of his apartment building, that I had made a mistake. Gary was not a man I fancied, for an array of reasons. For one thing, he was wearing slacks – chinos, I'm sure he would call them – and a shirt, perfectly pressed and buttoned almost to the neck. His apartment was decorated in various shades of greige; his sofa was black pleather.

He had the appearance of someone who'd been made all wrong. He had the rosy cheeks of a chubby toddler, accentuated by very round-framed glasses I felt sure his mother had picked out for him, and he was almost obscenely tall, wearing a tailored suit that I was sure cost more than anything I owned.

His housemate, he told me proudly, was gay (I'm sure this made him feel very forward-thinking) and, crucially, not at home. 'We have the place to ourselves.'

We ate the steak at his breakfast bar, perched on high stools, sipping wine from obnoxiously large wine glasses. The meat was tough and tasteless, served with boiled potatoes, which felt very on-brand for him. I chewed my steak and drank my wine and wondered how I might make my excuses. I could feign illness; I could pretend I'd got a call from a friend. Actually, I thought, I couldn't do either of those things. I had as good as promised to have sex with him – it was all there, in the sordid history of our Twitter messages.

After dinner, in one of the many awkward silences that arose when he stopped talking and I was busy racking my brains to figure out how to break my sex promise, he suggested we watch a movie.

We sat, side by side, on his pleather couch, not touching for the first – at least – thirty minutes, until he shifted his weight on to his left elbow and leaned on my leg, brushing the inside of my knee with the side of his thumb. He rubbed concentric circles on my leg for what felt like ten years before, all of a sudden, kissing me passionately, his tongue darting out from between his teeth and into my half-open mouth as I thought to myself, *you promised*.

I have never understood, really, why anyone ever suggests 'taking this to the bedroom' – but that is what he did after approximately three minutes of soft, fervent tongue kissing. He had gone to the trouble of telling me his housemate was out – why wouldn't we just have sex on the couch? Still, I did what he asked. It did not occur to me at any stage that evening *not* to do what he asked. I had promised.

On the side table beside his bed, he had a large bottle of lubricant – the kind you only buy when it's on offer because it costs about fifty quid otherwise. It was almost finished, a tragic final half-centimetre of gel at the bottom, waiting for its moment to shine.

To his credit, Gary was a very attentive lover. He is one of a handful of men who has bothered to go down on me until I achieved orgasm – although the fact that I did, with him, on that night, worries me sometimes. Is it a combination of self-loathing and horror that really allows me to slip off the edge? I hope not, but I wouldn't be surprised, because my own desire rarely seems to come into it. I get off on the idea that someone else wants *me*. I am the object, not the subject, of the interaction.

After I had come and he had told me – and I wish I could forget – that I tasted delicious, we had sex in the missionary position until he achieved orgasm, too. He kissed my shoulders and told me, 'That was wonderful, just wonderful.' For such a baby-faced twentysomething, he spoke – and dressed – like a middle-aged banker.

I got dressed quickly and told him I had to go home. He said I was welcome to stay but I shook my head no; I hadn't promised that. He walked me down to the door of his apartment building and he kissed me on the cheek and he said, 'Listen – don't take it the wrong way if you don't hear from me for a few weeks. I have a really busy period coming up with work and I'll probably be MIA.'

I think I just said 'grand'.

In reality, I was exceptionally relieved that his busy work schedule was going to get in the way of our budding romance, and didn't see it as quite the insulting brush-off I might have, had he been someone I was interested in seeing again. So you can imagine my surprise when he texted me that night, to ask if I'd got home and to tell me what a 'wonderful' time he'd had. (Again.) I told him I had got home, thanked him for the steak and told him I'd chat to him soon.

I heard from him again the following day, and the

day after that. Within a week, he'd asked me to go to dinner with him. When I asked him what had happened to his busy work schedule, he replied, without hesitation, 'Oh, I was just saying that to keep you keen.'

I told him, then, that I didn't think we were a good match. Behind the screen of my mobile phone, I was finally brave enough to say no to something I had previously said yes to. I told him I'd had a nice time. I told him I thought he was a lovely guy. Each of those things was at least partly true.

I next saw him at a Twitter meet-up about two months later, where I proceeded to get very drunk and kiss someone else in front of him. He messaged me later that night to tell me that he thought I'd treated him quite unfairly, that he'd really liked me and I'd hurt him. I still feel guilty when I remember that kiss, and those messages.

When I think back to the night I went for dinner – that steak, that lube, that orgasm – I feel like he was probably right. I did treat him unfairly. I should have been brave enough to be honest – to both him and myself.

I think I was just scared that, if I did tell him that I didn't want to give him what I'd promised, he'd press the issue until I gave in. And I knew from experience that I would, in fact, give in – and that, in giving in, I ran the risk of losing a part of myself, a part I felt I'd only recently won back. That wasn't his fault, but it wasn't quite mine, either.

Ed

For months after the smattering of dates I had with Ed, a marketing manager I'd met through my online life, I talked about him as if we'd had a serious relationship, one that he'd ended out of the blue, leaving me blindsided.

It was years – three, maybe four – before I realised that what we'd had, if anything, was a mild dalliance. We'd never gone for dinner. We'd never had a phone call. I don't feel as though either of those things is an essential foundation for a successful relationship, but it is important, I think, when telling this story, to be honest.

We first met at a networking event – something I would never go to now. For a while, though, in my early twenties, I was a big fan of these post-work shindigs, designed to bring media types together in whatever 'cool' new bar had just opened. There were always at least three free drinks, and there was always finger food, which is inevitably fried, my favourite method of food prep.

I remember it distinctly, even now. Ed was

sitting at the bar, slumped, slightly, over a pint of Guinness.

I would like to pause here to make a point about people who drink Guinness. It takes a certain constitution to have Guinness as your drink of choice. It is so *filling*, for one thing, but it's also just so distinctive. A night out drinking Guinness inevitably becomes about the drink itself. It's not the kind of beverage that fades into the background. No one who drinks Guinness would wake up the next morning and think, *What did I drink last night?*

Guinness colours everything it touches – the entire evening takes on the tone, the taste, the tang of hops. Guinness is the drink of someone who never answers a question with 'I don't mind', and I find that terrifying, if also kind of admirable.

My friend Dena knew Ed – she worked in advertising, at a firm that had done some work with his. I sat next to him at the bar, drank my drink – whatever complimentary cocktail was being proffered on trays – as we discussed the event, the industry, the day. To be honest, I don't remember our conversation, but I do remember the outline of him, the shape he made sitting on that stool.

He was – probably is – one of those people who has mastered the art of eye contact. I often think there are certain industries for which this skill is a prerequisite: marketing, for sure, but also TV and radio presenting, probably matchmaking, too. As we spoke that night, he made me feel like the most interesting person he'd ever met. He listened well and shared little, which reinforced the idea that he was absolutely captivated by me, while simultaneously making me think, *Here's someone mysterious*.

If I am ever tasked with writing a letter to my younger self, say, in a women's magazine feature about my life thus far, I will tell her that 99 per cent of all people who appear mysterious are, in fact, one-dimensional dullards who simply have nothing to contribute to the conversation. Imagine the time I could save myself.

Dena didn't know him all that well, but she was friends with one of his colleagues, and she was 'pretty sure' that he had a girlfriend. This was just typical: the first man I'd fancied in approximately three hours and he was already taken!

I saw him next at another marketing event, but this one was of his own making. He had tried to get a viral campaign going based around a mischievous cartoon dog, who'd been leaving clues all over the city as to what his ultimate end game was.

A group of us gathered outside a nondescript building before being ushered up the stairway into a Scandi-ly decorated three-bed apartment and treated to a presentation on all of the new innovations coming soon to Irish homes. I remember it as one of the most fun nights of my journalistic career thus far. A mystery! A man I fancied! Free drinks! Spring rolls! This would be hard to beat.

I was pretty confident, at that stage, that my feelings for Ed – I definitely fancied him, stalked his social media on a daily basis and had concluded that we had so much in common that we were essentially made for one another – were reciprocated, but his mysterious nature, coupled with the fact that we had exclusively spent time with one another in semi-professional (albeit boozy) settings, meant that I could come up with a plethora of excuses as to why he hadn't made any significant effort to flirt with (or even speak to) me.

Of course, there was also the matter of this mysterious girlfriend I had been told of, but who he had never brought up and who, if I tried hard enough, I could convince myself was of the past, and no longer someone I had to worry about.

There was something else about this particular period in 2010 that made this 'relationship' all the more intense to me: Foursquare. Foursquare was, and is, a location-sharing app that allows users to 'check in' to various locations, rate them and share recommendations with friends. It also gave awards and badges to users based on how often they checked in to specific locations. I was, at one stage, mayor of the newspaper I then worked at, a fact of which I was weirdly proud. I remember Foursquare being a feature of certain networking events; we'd be urged to check in, with the hope that, if enough of us did it, we'd get special event badges and awards. I suppose that was the start of the gamification of real life, and I was an enthusiastic player.

Ed was an active Foursquare user and so, of course, I became an active Foursquare user too, checking in furiously when I was anywhere I thought was 'of note'. This included – but was not limited to – cafés, restaurants, bars (especially bars, I wanted him to think I had an active social life) and my office at Ireland's 'paper of record'. 'Busy career woman and gal about town, Rosemary Mac Cabe,' was the bio I was hoping my Foursquare activity was subtly bestowing upon me.

I once even checked into Dublin's biggest maternity hospital; not knowing that it was specifically a maternity hospital, I thought it might make him wonder if everything was okay and that he might reach out, worried, to ensure I wasn't unwell. (I was having an ultrasound because my doctor thought that the strings of my IUD had recoiled up inside the opening of my cervix. They hadn't.)

The fact that Foursquare was experiencing a (short-lived) surge in popularity in this particular time is significant to this story because it gave me the ability to stalk this man in a way that I had never before been able to stalk anyone. (Thankfully, I have never again met anyone who was active on Foursquare and, once Ed and I were done, I had no need for it, so I deleted my account.)

The first time we kissed was on a night out in my honour, the day I finally arrived home from a trip I had taken to Granada, in the south of Spain. I had flown there for a five-day Spanish language course, expecting to fly back – but an Icelandic volcano had begun erupting, spewing ash high into the air and grounding flights in Europe and beyond.

The chaos at the bus station in Granada the following day was something I hope never to experience again. There were long lines of tourists vying for a spot on buses to London, Paris, Berlin, anywhere on a long list of cities whose airports were temporarily closed for business. People were shouting, crying and jostling for space in the crowd.

I got myself a seat on a bus to London, which was said to take twenty-six hours. From there, I would get the train to Wales, where I would board a ferry to Ireland.

With an hour left to board my bus, I had wandered off to find a newsagent, where I hoped to stock up on snacks for the journey. I found a bodega staffed by a large, tanned man who had, at some point in his life, decided to have his eyeliner tattooed on. It gave him a startled, but also kind of piercing, look.

My Spanish was rudimentary – although better than it had been five days previously, let me tell you – and I struggled to ask for what I needed. I was confused by the foreign snack selection and just wanted to find some semi-healthy forms of sustenance to tide me over until I made it home in a day or so.

'I'm taking a ... long journey,' I told him in my pidgin Spanish. 'I am looking for some snacks. Bars of cereal or ... something. I'm taking a long journey. I need food for the bus.'

He looked me up and down and wiggled his index finger at me as he spoke. 'Honey – you've got reserves.'

When I looked shocked and probably insulted, he

corrected himself, saying, 'I like it!' I did not feel reassured.

The bus took forty-two hours in total, and I made an early error of revealing to my fellow passengers that I spoke Spanish, thereby becoming the journey's spokeswoman, tasked with asking the driver, every hour or so, how long we had left or whether or not we'd be stopping soon to use the loo. To his unending credit, he had the patience of a saint – something I remind myself of whenever I find myself in the car with a child who simply must know if we are nearly there yet every five minutes.

While on the voyage, I – of course – tweeted my progress, something that got picked up by several news outlets who called me, while en route, to discuss my great journey across the European continent. The hashtag #bringrosemaryhome trended on Twitter.

The morning I arrived off the boat in Dublin, Dena picked me up at the port and drove me home. I slept for six hours and then got up, showered and dressed myself for a night out to celebrate my homecoming.

A handful of Twitter friends showed up to buy me drinks and be regaled with tales of tattooed eyeliner and bus sing-songs, Ed among them, and we all ended up in a nightclub around the corner, dancing to Weezer and drinking pints. It should not surprise you to know that, occasionally, when trying to impress a man, I still drink pints.

Towards the end of the night, Ed and I found ourselves alone at the end of the bar nearest the door – closest to the escape route – kissing passionately.

The feeling of kissing someone you've fancied for ages is, in my books, almost unrivalled. It's like a magical combination of goal achievement and wish fulfilment and romantic destiny. I distinctly remember the breath leaving my body as I melted into him and thought, *Finally*, and probably, if I'm honest, *This is it. True love.*

It is a truth universally acknowledged that all stories of true love begin with a man being so drunk that he can't sustain an erection, so I took him home and we did not have sex but kissed some more and I thought, *poor him*.

I didn't hear from him for a few weeks after that night, although I'm sure I sent him at least three extremely nonchalant text messages asking how he was, making some joke about how drunk we were, suggesting – casually – that we meet up. He was fine, yes we were (lol), he was busy.

If there was a message being sent, I most certainly was not getting it. *Poor him*, I thought, *he's very busy at work*.

In the meantime, Dena had confirmed to me that he did, in fact, have a long-term American girlfriend, who had returned to the US and with whom he was in a long-distance relationship. I wouldn't have fully believed her if it hadn't been confirmed by another Twitter friend of ours, who just happened to be in a long-term relationship with Ed's sister. Ireland is always just small enough for any kind of secret-keeping to be untenable.

I asked him about his girlfriend the next time we

met, at a digital awards event I was attending as one half of a nominated podcast – at the time, I co-presented a podcast about TV with my cousin, Roseanne, called, fittingly, *The Rosie View* – and he was attending as part of his work. He told me they'd broken up.

I'm not sure whether or not he acknowledged that he had cheated on her when we'd spent that night together a few weeks previously, or whether or not he apologised, but the fact that I can't remember probably belies the truth of it: I didn't really care. He was free now, and would surely – surely! – soon be with me.

I went home with him that night, to an apartment I would come to fantasise about very frequently – oh, the things I would do with his decor! – and we had sex, although, again, not without a little trouble. I tried not to take it personally (reader, I failed) and made up for it by giving him three blow jobs through-out the night. Every time either of us stirred, I'd lob his dick in my mouth as if to say, *Look how sexual I am! I just want to pleeeeeeease you!*

The following day, *incredibly* hungover, I texted him and asked if he'd like to go to the cinema 'and not talk' (see? Very 'cool girl' of me, I know what men want). He stayed over at mine afterwards, on what would be the only sober night we'd spend together.

The following day, he called me – called me! – to tell me that he had chlamydia, and I should probably get checked. He apologised and I said, in the style of a cool girl, 'Don't apologise! We both had unprotected sex! It's no more your fault than it is mine!' and made an appointment with my doctor to be treated for an STI I wasn't sure I had (but better safe than sorry).

After that, I didn't hear from him for several weeks bar the odd text exchange which I would initiate and he would, inevitably, end by simply *not* writing back.

The last time we met was for a post-work drink, suggested by me; we didn't go home together afterwards, probably because the night was still young and we both felt too awkward to suggest it. In my mind, this was the first 'proper' date we'd gone on, and surely the start of something wonderful – *especially* because it hadn't ended in sex. Surely this was because our 'relationship' was starting to *mean* something to him.

This is going to shock you, so please, take a moment to prepare yourself: he was not biding his time, or playing it cool, or any combination of the two. I didn't hear from him.

The closest I got was when Dena met him at a work event around six months later and brought me up in conversation – Dena is the kind of friend who is loyal almost to a fault, and will always have your best interests at heart. She relayed to me, afterwards, that she basically told him to stop 'dicking me around', and asked him what he was playing at.

He told her that he really liked me, and asked if she thought he'd fucked things up. Dena, to her credit, didn't tell him the truth – that of course he hadn't fucked things up, that I was simply *waiting* for him to come to his senses – but suggested that, if he really wanted any kind of relationship with me, he should put in some effort.

The only mistake Dena made, honestly, is that she immediately relayed this conversation to me. If kissing Ed after weeks of fancying him was one of the best feelings of my life, this was a close second. *He really, really liked me!* I was overjoyed. And the timing couldn't have been better; I had a spare ticket to a music festival in Dublin city centre that weekend that I was planning on offering to a friend but now I had a much better prospect! (Sorry, Clare.)

At this stage of our back-and-forth, there was no point in making any effort to be casual or laid-back about it. We were past that, I thought, happily. We both really, *really* liked each other!

I texted him and told him I had a spare ticket, asked if he'd like to come. As it happens, he was already going – but thanks! I suggested we meet at some stage over the weekend (casual! cool!) for a drink. 'Sure,' he replied, which, to my mind, was an enthusiastic yes. It was practically a date!

This actually *will* be a surprise – it was to me – but I didn't text him all weekend, waiting, instead, for him to get in touch to meet me for that drink we'd discussed. There was no word until, on Sunday night, fifteen minutes after the last act had ended, as we were all making our way home, walking down the long driveway of the Irish Museum of Modern Art and heading towards the city, hoping to get a bus or a tram home, I got a text.

'Hey. A few of us going back to mine for some [emoji largely known to mean cocaine]. Wanna come?'

I was livid. Do I want to come to his apartment *with a group of people I don't know* to do cocaine?! This was not how great romances were born.

That was the first moment – and as I recount all of this, I think, *how?!* – that I saw clearly how little interest he had in me, really. I didn't quite understand that you could really *like* someone and *not* want to date them, or be otherwise romantically involved with them.

I think, for him, I probably had the potential to be a fun, casual fling, until it became very clear that I was not the type. It was through my persistence alone that the whole thing dragged on far longer than it should have.

I replied to him, finally tossing aside all notions of being cool, casual or in any way laid-back. 'Never contact me again,' I told him. 'Delete my number.'

That would have been a good place for our little dalliance to end, and it is tempting to leave it there, to insert a musical coda and move on. But, sadly, that's not where it ended – at least not for me.

I thought about him almost every day for weeks afterwards. He had fucked things up, yes, but so had I, by reacting in such an over-the-top fashion to his friendly suggestion of some group drug-taking. Why was I so *uncool*?!

I kept wishing I'd bump into him around town so

that I could, once again, pretend to be cool and drink pints and make him see what it was that he liked about me.

Instead, several weeks later, I texted him asking if we could 'start over'. (Why had I kept his number? Could it be that I knew I would, one day, come crawling back?!)

'What do you mean?' he asked, obtusely. 'Sure we can be friends!'

'No,' I said, clearly absolutely incapable of reading on the lines themselves, never mind between them. 'I mean, start over, go on a date.'

He never wrote back.

Frank

I have never been someone who thinks that women and men can't be friends – that is, *just friends*. I have, like most women my age, I'd guess, read magazine column after magazine column positing that, in heterosexual, opposite-sex friendships, there is always someone who wishes it were more than 'just' a friendship, that the sentiments are never equal on both sides, and still, I don't believe that to be true.

And yet.

Frank and I met through work, where, in my experience, no romance should ever start. We worked in adjacent buildings, and semi-related professions – I was working in journalism, he in PR – and we started to spend time together as I became good friends with a woman who worked at the desk next to mine. She and Frank had been besties for years, and she invited me to tag along on their work lunches.

I'm not quite sure what we had in common, with the exception of our work, which was only vaguely related, really – but at the time, that was probably enough. We frequently found ourselves at the same events, where we would stand at the bar and gossip about who was clearly blanking who, or how terrible the product whose launch we were here to herald was. I was twenty-six at the time; he was in his early forties and married, with three small children.

As an aside: I've always wondered if it is the 'other woman' who is having an affair, per se, or if it is just the man. If I am single, can it be an affair? Is just one person having the affair, and the other person having a relationship? Perhaps that answers my question, because it definitely wasn't a relationship, although I tried to convince myself, at the time, that it was.

Before the first night we kissed and went home together and had terrible drunken sex – sex that was not worth the strife or the guilt or the embarrassment – I can honestly say, hand on heart, that it was not a scenario I had ever thought about. As far as I knew, he was happily married, and I was not the type of girl to sleep with a married man.

We were at – of course – a work event that had got boozier and boozier as the night wore on, and when that event ended, we decided to continue the night in a nearby nightclub, an infamous Dublin spot that was renowned as somewhere you'd go to get drunk, or laid, or both.

My friend Roisin had, coincidentally, been at the event, and came to the club with us, but as soon as we walked through the doors we lost her in the throng. She is the type of person who will always bump into someone she knows and, sure enough, she had met a friend of a friend and then gone downstairs with them to say hi to someone else they both knew.

We stood at the bar and marvelled at the bizarre circumstance in which we found ourselves – surrounded by teenagers, in a club I had been to once and whose interior he hadn't seen in over a decade. A drunk, ruddy-faced twentysomething approached us and asked if he'd seen me on the telly.

'Probably,' I told him, laughing, then turned away. I wasn't quite drunk enough to want to start a detailed conversation with a stranger about my life on screen, which functioned as a sort of spin-off of my journalism career and involved random, sporadic appearances on evening talk shows detailing new trends or debating women's issues on an afternoon panel programme I occasionally guested on.

It happened in what felt like a haze: we were standing at the bar and we were talking and we were ordering drinks and we were kissing, and there is no moment, in my memory, that separates any of those actions, or in which a different choice could have been made. One thing, as they say, led to another.

Frank came home with me that night and we had very bad, very drunk sex, the kind of sex where you're not quite sure what's going on, or where. It was as if neither of us had ever *had* sex before. Buttons were newfangled inventions, impossible to navigate. My bra clasp? Forget it, I kept it on.

The following morning, I was incredulous, tinged with the kind of delight I always felt on the morning after some sexscapade or other.

In a way, that affair marked a kind of split in my sense of self – or, at the very least, in how I viewed the world. In the years before, I thought there were two types of women: women who had affairs – slightly pathetic and definitely desperate – and women who didn't. Pre-affair, I would have firmly placed myself in the second category.

For the six months we were seeing one another, I believed in pretty much the same basic structure, with the significant difference being that I had moved from category two to category one and was, therefore, desperate, lonely and pathetic. Post-affair, nothing was quite so simple. I now know that women who have affairs can be pathetic and desperate, sure, but also self-respecting and hopeful and loving and caring – or all (or none) of the above. There is no common denominator.

Of all the relationships I've had, none has made me feel quite as alone as that one did. It took over my life. It eclipsed all others.

I became, for the first time, a liar. It wasn't so much compulsive as it was necessary. I lied to everyone about everything – about who I'd had lunch with, about where I was going tonight, about whether or not I was single (was I?), about what I'd be doing this weekend, or the next.

Frank would come over and I would put my phone on flight mode and tell my friends I was out with other friends, or at the movies, or at a concert (and hope they'd never ask for details) and we'd eat take-out and have sex and, later – but never too late – he'd get up and he'd get dressed and he'd go home and I would tidy away the takeout containers and the condoms and the blanket we'd been lying under on the couch. I'd reactivate my network and I would wait for a flurry of texts and the silence would always be ever so slightly disappointing. Sure, I'd told them I was busy, but still, it rankled.

The lying, aside from being an isolating experience, made me feel like I had become someone else entirely. I had never been someone who lied. I had never been someone who *could* lie. I told the truth, for better or worse. I was – I am – an excessive over-sharer.

I was someone who would call friends and give them a blow-by-blow account of my day, or my night. I would tell them the details of my other friendships and my work relationships and talk about what book I was reading and what film I had seen. I would spare no details in my confessional, regular chats.

During the affair, well, there was no point calling anyone. I couldn't tell them about my life. What would I have to talk about? Discussing events that are made up is incredibly boring for everyone involved. If I couldn't talk about Frank, I had nothing to talk about; as he was all I wanted to talk about, he became the only person I talked to.

It didn't really occur to me at the time, because it felt like we were both in it – in this space, this relationship we'd made in my house, alone – but really, I was the only one who was truly alone. Frank had his family and his friends and a life with his wife. I had pulled away from friends and family so that I could protect my secret, while he had to stay close to his, for the exact same reason. In my isolation, I needed him. I think he probably liked it that way.

I tried to end things a couple of times, half-heartedly, kind of like I regularly tried to quit smoking. I knew it was bad for me. I knew it wouldn't end well. I knew I'd be better off without him and that he needed space to deal with what he had going on in his life. He wasn't sleeping, he told me; he had chronic back pain; he'd had a headache for weeks. His body was, I thought, manifesting the symptoms of his guilt.

As for me, it wasn't really guilt that I was feeling. I've always thought it is the married party who should feel the guilt and that, if there is shame, it is theirs alone. I do feel ashamed, now – less because he was married and more because, with the benefit of hindsight, my motivations seem so transparent. I was amazed that someone like him – someone older, someone smarter, someone more popular and better known and more sociable and, ultimately, better than me – would risk disrupting the pattern of his life. For me. At the time, it felt like a compliment. I drank it up.

When things finally – inevitably – came to an end, I'd spent six months avoiding my friends. I'd spent six months lying to my parents and my sister about what I was doing on any given evening. I'd spent six months hiding away with this man who told me something had to change; he didn't want the life he had built for himself and he wanted something else. Something more. I thought that included me.

He ended our affair in the snow. We had gone to a bar for a few drinks one weekday evening. We could do that because we had, before all of this happened, been friends. His wife, he'd told me, wanted me to come over for dinner. I imagined the conversation. 'It sounds like you're really friendly with Rosemary – why don't you invite her over? Is she seeing anyone? Maybe she could bring him.'

After we'd finished our last drink – I drank vodka then, with Diet Coke or a dash of lime (depending on who was paying) – Frank walked me the three blocks up the street to my house. The snow had been falling for days; as it melted and refroze, my kitchen ceiling started to leak, a slow drip of ice-cold water coming down through the flat roof.

People had tried to tidy up the streets but they didn't quite know how to. We don't have snow ploughs in Ireland and, in their absence, decisions had to be made. A kind of disorganised shovelling had been agreed upon, leaving enormous mounds of dirty snow piled at regular intervals on the path. They looked like giant snowmen who'd started to thaw and then frozen once more, having lost all shape and appearance of life.

He told me it had to finish. It was bad for him. It wouldn't end well. He needed to sort out his life and his marriage and go home. I think I laughed; we'd had this conversation before, but the other way around, and he'd always talked me out of it. 'I know it has to stop,' he'd say. 'But we're having too much fun – it can't end now.' (I was easily convinced.)

I thought that we were just switching roles. I was

to take the reins, to deny him his moment of right-eousness. It was important that he felt like he was trying to do the right thing. But it couldn't end; we were having too much fun.

I probably told him not to be ridiculous. 'Come on, just come home with me and we'll talk.' But whatever had happened, whoever's advice he'd finally decided to heed (his own? Someone else's?), his mind was made up. He left me on the corner and I walked home, through the snow, to the house where I lived alone – where I'd moved largely because I hadn't wanted to take my married man home to my house-mates – to my two cats, who would soon retire to the country to live with my parents (but not before con-suming an entire budgie on the living room floor), to my phone, which showed no messages, no missed calls.

I'm not sure quite how long it took him to do what he said he would, and sort his life out – a few weeks, perhaps a few months, definitely less than a year. He left his wife, just like he said he would, and moved out, just like he said he would. He moved in with his new girlfriend (just like he said he would, when I was his girlfriend, when I thought he would be moving in with me). They adopted a dog – a little terrier with a bad hind leg – and, a year later, they welcomed a baby boy named Sonny.

I know all of these things from social media, and friends of friends, and nights out with people who know me and know him but don't know us, and so feel he is the common thread to stitch our conversa-tions together.

As for the two of us, we were never really friends after that night in the snow. In the immediate aftermath, I struggled massively with my mental health. I don't want to assign blame, because I've endured such events – long months of sadness and low mood and lack of motivation – since. I had endured them before him, too. But it turned out that he didn't really want to be my friend if we weren't having fun, and I didn't really know how to have fun with him if we weren't together.

We stopped having lunch together. We stopped texting and responding to each other's tweets and then, one day, he passed me on the street and we didn't even say hello.

It's as if none of it ever happened. I put on the fur coat and went through the wardrobe and was back in a flash, a little wiser and a little lonelier and, for the first time in my life, hating the snow.

Liam

I met Liam in my house, which is, when you think about it, a weird place to meet someone for the first time. He was a friend of my then housemate Regan, and would regularly appear in our living room on a Saturday or Sunday morning.

He was then living with his parents, an hour's train ride outside Dublin, and would frequently call Regan at an ungodly hour to ask if he could stay over after a night out that had ended well after the last train left the station. I would hear him arrive – he is not, and I hope this is not news to him, a good whisperer – and begin to regale Regan with tales of his night's shenanigans.

Liam is the kind of person everyone likes, a quality that he miraculously manages to hold on to when he is drunk. Sober, he is polite and friendly; he is incredibly interested in any new people he meets, and asks just enough flattering questions – 'Did you make that yourself, it's amazing!' – to find some common ground upon which to build what can only be called 'a good chat'.

I have only ever known one person to dislike

Liam – we'll get to that later – and even then, that was through no fault of Liam's own.

At the time, he was working in a supermarket 'down home' while also doing the odd bit of free-lance reporting for a culture show on RTÉ radio and, at weekends, performing on stage in Bunny's Hutch, a weekly variety show in the basement of Pantibar, one of Dublin's most popular gay bars.

Having been a Muppet-obsessed child, Liam had, instead of growing out of his love of puppets, chosen to grow *into* it, amassing quite the collection of Henson Studios creations and becoming a self-taught master puppeteer. He and his puppets would mime along to songs from the musicals: 'If You Were Gay', from *Avenue Q*, was a firm crowd-pleaser, while 'Baptize Me' from *The Book of Mormon* included an excellent on-stage gag that involved squirting water from a squeezy bottle on to Bunny herself, the drag queen host of the night.

We had spent a not inconsiderable amount of time together – eating breakfast, walking into town together after a night out (his), chatting around the television – by the time we went on our first official 'date', for coffee (me) and tea (him), to Fallon & Byrne, a kind of upmarket food-hall-slash-supermarket-slash-restaurant in town.

We sat on high stools and I took a photograph of him in the afternoon light that streamed in through the windows and I thought that I had never met someone quite as lovely as he was. I was going to meet friends afterwards, and he came with me; we drank in the beer garden of that bar until closing time and we stumbled home, laughing at the circumstances that brought him to Regan's door tonight, so different to all of those other nights.

We kissed in the doorway of the little terraced house and I invited him inside. My bedroom was in the front of the house, with my double bed up on a platform, accessed by a little ladder. It was a smart design, making the most of the space in the small room, but when you were drunk it was, of course, perilous, to say the least. That was the first night Liam would fall down the ladder leading up to my bed, but not the last.

It's fair to say that I have never been a particularly slow mover when it comes to romantic relationships, but with Liam any tendencies I had towards gameplaying or cool-girl roleplay were thrown out the window.

It was obvious that he really liked me. In fact, I had known since before we went on that first date, when I woke up one night at 3 a.m. to him and Regan arguing in the living room.

'Just let me go in and say *hi*! She won't mind!' said Liam, pissed and slurring his words ever so slightly.

'Liam. Absolutely not. Come on now, it's time to go to bed,' Regan replied patiently, in a stern-but-fair teacherly tone.

'Butilikehersomuch!' Liam slurred in protest.

Two weeks after that first date, I invited him to come as my plus-one to a press event in Bath, in the UK, for the release of some incredibly dull study by

Procter & Gamble. They had booked out Babington House, an exceptionally posh and somewhat exclusive hotel in a listed manor house with its own private lake, perhaps to make up for the boredom of the presentations we were about to endure, and told us to bring our other halves.

At that point, he wasn't my other half, and I'll admit that, in asking him, I was a bit worried that I was being too *keen*, but I needn't have worried: Liam is a sensible chap who loves a freebie, especially when said freebie involves a weekend away in a luxury hotel.

We flew to London City Airport and from there met our group at Paddington Station. Liam asked me to take a photograph of him with the statue of Paddington Bear, one of his favourite childhood characters. When we reached Babington House, we frolicked around the room, taking photographs of one another lounging on the four-poster bed.

It wasn't a purely idyllic weekend; I had a bad cold and ended up taking to bed right after dinner. Liam, a social animal, stayed at the bar chatting to the other journalists who were on the trip: a writer for *GQ*, another for British *Vogue*, a man who worked at *Esquire* and wore skinny jeans, brogues and no socks. When the bar closed, Liam later reported to me, one of them – probably Boris or Edmund or Roger – had told him, in no uncertain terms, that they were going to his room to continue the night, and that he was *not* invited.

I was unsurprised, not necessarily that they hadn't

wanted to hang out with Liam, although I will admit that he had been taking liberal advantage of the free bar and was quite possibly in a different place, at least metaphorically, than they were, but that they were rude. My experience with glossy magazine journalists in the UK had taught me to expect as much.

The Irish media world is small and tight-knit; people move from one magazine to another, and remain friends with the colleagues they left behind. We will happily share taxis and lipsticks and fix one another's eyeliner in the bathroom.

In the UK media world – in London, more specifically – journalists from *Vogue* will not share a taxi with journalists from *Elle*. *This* beauty writer will not attend an event if *that* fashion editor is there. One of my favourite stories about the London glossies involves a features editor asking her assistant to return a bunch of flowers to a PR who was thanking her for including their client in the latest issue.

'I'm sorry, but she hates flowers,' the assistant was purported to have said. 'She only accepts gift cards – and Moët.'

I think, had I been in Babington House alone, I would have found these journalists intimidating. I'd been at the *Irish Times* for a few years at this stage, and wrote almost exclusively about fashion and lifestyle, so I'd had more than a few interactions with the UK press, but the men were new to me, and if I'd found the women aloof and intimidating, these fashionable fellows were like a superior alien race I could never hope to befriend or even understand.

But with Liam by my side, it became clear that whatever stand-offishness they had chosen to display was *their* problem.

'How can they be pissed off?!' he asked, when he overheard one of them complaining about his coffee being cold. 'This place is *amazing*!'

It's true that press freebies can often inoculate you to just how lucky you are, and how lovely the experience you're having is (without even having to pay for it!), but with Liam by my side everything seemed more fun.

By the time we got home, we were boyfriend and girlfriend. It was a quick escalation, but there was very little fuss or fanfare about the adjustment of our relationship status: it just seemed to make sense, and Liam was very forthright about things like that. Neither of us was interested in dating anyone else, and we were both happy to admit that we were mad about each other.

The start of our relationship coincided with a difficult period for me at work. I was grappling with my relationship with my manager; things had started out positively, but soured over time, and I was finding myself increasingly anxious about going into the office, never knowing what mood they would be in, or how that mood would affect their behaviour towards me.

I started attending weekly therapy sessions, in an effort to deal with the feeling of terror – job-interview jitters, as I described them – that had started to show up in the pit of my stomach every morning before work, as I struggled to figure out whether keeping my job was worth losing my sanity.

A few months after we'd started dating, I broke up with Liam, more or less out of the blue. I had been in a state of high stress related to work for what felt like weeks, and I had also started to branch out slightly, picking up different odd jobs in the hopes of cutting down my office-based shifts and, therefore, getting out from under my manager's clutches.

As a result, my calendar was filling up to what felt like untenable levels, and I distinctly remember thinking about the next few weeks and being unable to find a gap in which I could catch my breath, sit on the couch and mindlessly watch reality TV while playing *Candy Crush* on my phone.

The one thing I could think of that could easily be removed – I couldn't cancel these jobs I had lined up, and calling in sick to work because of my mental health?! As if! – was my relationship with Liam. He was still working weekends at the supermarket, but during the week he would stay with me for two or three nights – his being friends with my housemate was a great advantage that meant Regan was unlikely to complain about our newly crowded house – and I suddenly felt as though, if I could reclaim those nights for myself, I could somehow clear out the fog of anxiety that was descending over me.

I broke up with him on a Sunday, on a visit to his parents' house while they were out at the races. In terms of reasoning, I had very little to give him; I could only say, feebly, that I didn't think it was going to work out. He began to cry and turned his back to me. When I went to let myself out the front door, I had to call him to unlock it as I couldn't quite figure out the latch.

By the following afternoon, I had realised my error. Of *all* the things I could choose to cancel on my calendar, I chose *Liam*?! I tried to call him and explain, but he wouldn't speak to me, telling me he needed to take some time to clear his head.

So I did what any reasonable person would do, plagued with guilt and in a panic that I had lost the best thing to ever happen to me: I adopted a puppy. A Facebook friend of mine's dog had become better acquainted than anyone had expected with the dog next door, and they had six pups looking for good homes. I snapped one up and called her Coileán, the Irish for 'puppy'.

When, the following week, I went to meet Liam to beg for his forgiveness, I brought Coileán – then the size of a Beanie Baby – along, thinking, honestly, that she would provide a great ice-breaker and focal point, should the conversation remain as chilly as our recent text exchanges.

Whether it was the tiny puppy or my personal charms, Liam forgave me my lapse in judgement and we were back on. But he felt more delicate than before, as if I'd suddenly realised that he was break-able, and I was careful, in the ensuing weeks, to treat him as though he was precious, and not something I could simply wipe off my calendar in order to allevi-ate my stress.

I never did quite solve my manager problem. I saw a few different therapists, ending up on medication for generalised depressive disorder, a decision that has served me well over the past decade or so. I gradually moved into more and more freelance work and out of the office; I learned not to fill my calendar so full that I cannot see a gap or a day off in my immediate future.

I still go through periods of feeling anxious, stressed and sad, and I try to cope with them as best I can. Sometimes I cry in the car. Sometimes I cancel plans and I hope that people will understand. (Sometimes they don't.) It's all trial and error.

Shortly after that mini-breakup, Liam and I decided to move in together – like I said, I've never been a slow mover – and began to look for a house in Dublin for the three of us. It's always difficult to find a rental place that will let you have a dog, never mind a rental place that's *suitable* for a dog, but we found a house with a little garden about five minutes' walk from the city centre and registered our interest.

Liam was then doing more and more work with RTÉ, and even though I was branching out a bit, I was still working as a journalist, and honestly I think our jobs had a lot to do with our landlord accepting us. That, and the fact that we told her our dog was 'small', five years old, and fully house-trained.

Coileán was of course then less than four months old and small only because of her age – she would end up medium in size, about the size of a beagle – but she was a good girl when it came to her toilet habits, so on that front at least we told the truth.

As short as it was, relatively speaking – we were together for a little over a year, in all – my relationship with Liam was one of the best I've ever had. We were best friends, in the true sense of the term: there was nothing we didn't, or couldn't, talk about with one another, from past relationships to our hopes and dreams, our likes and dislikes, the worries we had about our futures and careers and even the kinds of ridiculous thoughts we sometimes had that we couldn't share with anyone else, for fear of seeming deeply stupid (more me than him, honestly).

We introduced one another to our innermost worlds, rewatching our favourite childhood movies and decorating our home with art depicting the nostalgia that made up each of our childhoods.

We invited friends over for dinner, where Coileán would lay her head on their laps as they ate, begging for scraps; we went out together, to the theatre and the museum and the art gallery nearby. And we laughed a lot, at one another (lovingly) but also *with* one another.

It didn't take long, really, for us both to recognise the fact that we were best friends. I would almost go as far as to say that we were soulmates. I can't imagine my life without Liam in it; I hope he feels the same way. (I don't want to know if he doesn't.)

As strong as our relationship was – and is, to this day – the romantic aspect, which had been so very present in the beginning, had almost entirely faded by the time we hit the one-year mark. We had long discussions about how we could remedy this – was it a phase? Could we to-do list our way out of it? – even talking about the possibility of having an open relationship, fulfilling our sexual needs outside of the two of us while living this life we both loved, together.

But I am not an open relationship type of person. It wasn't that I couldn't abide the idea of Liam sleeping with someone else, it was that I knew I would want to know every single detail, and that I would then use those details as a stick with which to beat myself. Were they thinner than me? More adventurous than me? A better kisser? Funnier than me? The possibilities with which to unfavourably compare myself were endless, and I didn't think that would be a good step for us in the long run.

At a friend's wedding, we tearfully discussed our inevitable breakup on the dance floor, his hands on my waist and mine around his neck, resting my head on his shoulder. In a way, the idea of *not* being together was unfathomable – but we agreed that we both deserved a relationship in which our wants and needs were fully met by the other person, rather than this incredible friendship that no longer seemed to hold any semblance of passion or desire.

We didn't break up that night, but a few weeks later we sat down on the side of our bed and made the decision we'd both been putting off. 'We'll still be best friends,' we promised one another, although I'm not sure if either of us quite believed it was possible at the time.

As he had done the first time I broke up with him, Liam started to cry and turned away from me – but this time, I was crying too. I lay down behind him and wrapped my arms around him, and we stayed there until we both fell asleep.

In the months after our mutually-agreed-upon breakup, Liam and I weren't quite friends. It took us a while to disentangle our lives – it took him a few weeks to find a place to move into, and I, no longer his girlfriend, suddenly stopped including him in my laundry schedule, or thinking of him when it came to dinner plans.

I would then get enraged at the sight of his over-flowing dirty clothes hamper, but feel as though I no longer had any 'right' to say anything. I couldn't wait for him to leave.

It wasn't until some time later, when the dust had settled and we had managed to reconfigure ourselves as people who could – and should – exist without one another, that we tentatively began to spend time together. A coffee here, a cinema date there.

Now, more than ten years on, we speak to one another several times a day. He produces my podcast. I proofread his writing. He is the first person I go to when I have a problem that I can't solve, or when I am arguing with my husband. He asks my advice when he is trying to figure out how to handle a blip in a working relationship, or when he can't figure out how to update his website.

I used to say I wished we had never dated. I used to think I had mistaken this incredible connection we undoubtedly have for something more romantic. But now I think it might be better this way.

I'll never wonder whether or not we'd make a good couple, because I know the answer: we made a great one. And we threw the best dinner parties.

Scott

Some relationships are harder to write about than others, for reasons that seem obvious and, sometimes, for reasons that seem less obvious. The obvious reason is that this relationship lasted half a decade. I spent five years thinking this was the man I would spend my life with, that this was the man I would make a family with.

The other reasons are that I'm not really sure, now, looking back, what brought us together – nor am I sure what drove us apart. It feels like there was very little driving us in either direction, except, perhaps, sheer force of will.

I met Scott when I was twenty-seven; he was twenty-three, although he told me he was twenty-four. We both started out that relationship lying – him about his age, and me about the time that had elapsed between my last relationship and this one, about the days I'd spent single, mourning the end of a relationship that had given me a best friend, a house, a dog and a collection of bespoke artworks modelled after my own face.

It wasn't so much a lie as it was my attempt to fudge the truth. We'd been broken up 'for a while', I told him, which was true, in a way, if 'a while' could be taken to mean two weeks and not, say, the twelve I was hoping he'd assumed it meant.

I was still living with Liam at the time, sleeping on the couch in our shared house because he had a bad back and had to sleep in the king-sized bed. My friend Ciara was renting our spare room, but I couldn't share with her because she had a new boyfriend and he was staying over a lot.

I was on my first night out since the breakup. Friends of friends were having Friday night drinks of a celebratory kind – a birthday, perhaps, or an engagement – in a newly opened five-star hotel near my house. We swigged Prosecco and listened to a Ladies' Night playlist on Spotify while we got ready.

I have photographs of that night – me, wearing Ciara's dress, with backcombed hair and fuchsia lipstick; the gals, posing for selfies like we used to when we cared about taking photographs with other people, and not just of ourselves. (Now, my phone memory is three-quarters full of photographs of myself, taken from a variety of angles, in different lighting. The other quarter is my son – I'm not entirely self-obsessed.)

Clare and I – we've been friends since meeting, at the age of four, in the Irish-language playschool my mother ran – had recently taken a course in burlesque. I had lied to everyone I knew, and myself, I suppose, in telling them that it was meant to be a great workout. To be honest, it was because I had just seen the film *Burlesque*, starring Cher and Christina Aguilera (in a terrible wig), and I just wanted to be sexy, like a cat, but wearing lingerie and high heels. I did learn to remove a pair of silk gloves with my teeth, but anything more than that was, I am sad to report, beyond me.

The studio was mirrored, which added insult to injury. Without them, I think, I could happily have shimmied and sashayed away, in the mistaken belief that I was doing 'it' right – being sexy, walking seductively and in time to the music – but there was no avoiding the glare of my reflection. Next to a half-dozen other women walking the same walk, shimmying the same shimmy, my distinct lack of grace was all too apparent.

As it turns out, all I needed was a few stiff drinks, because after a scattering of Proseccos and several expensive gin and tonics, quaffed on the rooftop of the latest 'place to be', Clare and I began to show off our newly acquired skills. We walked in tandem, and I was right – without the mirrors to shame me with a vision of my true self, I was a goddess. I was Julianne Hough, or (a much younger) Cher, removing an invisible glove to the beat of the music with glistening, pearly-white teeth.

Scott approached with a friend – asking, I think, what it was that we were doing. At the time I thought they were asking in admiration, in awe. 'Where did you learn to do such a thing?!' I imagined them asking us. The reality was, I'm sure, slightly more pedestrian. 'What are you *doing*?!' could be interpreted as admiring, bemused or, I dread to think, horrified.

We ended up spending the whole evening together, discussing the kinds of things I used to bring up to impress men – *Star Wars*, mainly – moving closer to one another at the bar until, finally, at the behest of a friend of his ('Are you guys *ever* going to kiss?!') we finally locked lips, sliding hands around one another's waists, threading our fingers through each other's hair (my backcombing made this challenging, to say the least).

When the end of the night came, not long after that moment, he asked me to go home with him. He was living with his mum, he told me, but she was 'really cool – she won't care if you come home with me'. I imagined some unusual circumstances that had resulted in them selling the family home, moving into a modern, two-bed apartment near the city centre. It would be like a bachelor pad, I thought, with his young, hip mum leading her young, hip life.

Of course, like my burlesque performance, the truth was far more pedestrian. The house was, in fact, his family home – a four-bedroom, semi-detached red-brick in the suburbs. The stairs were lined with photographs of him and his siblings at significant life moments. There was a bright Red Devil teddy bear in his bedroom, a mascot from his favourite football team, that I laughed at, which seemed to embarrass him – in the moment, it didn't occur to me that this was an unusual occurrence for him, that he didn't bring women home to his mum's house on the reg, sneaking them up the carpeted stairs past the ghosts of family Christmases past.

When I took off my clothes – Ciara's dress, black tights, the highest heels I owned and a black bodysuit I used to wear because it smoothed my lines and flattened my stomach – he told me, 'You have an incredible body.' I would remember those words a lot, in the five years following, because he would never compliment my body again.

Sure, he would tell me I looked nice – 'You look nice!' – or that he liked my hair, but he would never again look at my naked body and seem awestruck, or impressed, or even like he thought it was beautiful. In a way, I wish he'd never said it at all, not even that one time. You can't miss what you've never had.

We had quiet, awkward sex that didn't quite do the trick for either of us and then slept in his single bed, our bodies pressed tightly against one another. When we woke up the following morning, he told me to be quiet – in the harsh light of day, as it turns out, his mum wasn't as relaxed about his nocturnal adventures as he had told me. We waited to slip out until she had left for Saturday morning golf. I put back on my tights, my bodysuit, Ciara's dress, my impossibly high shoes, and he drove me home in the car he shared with his younger sister.

I kind of knew, when we said goodbye at the end of my street, as I kissed him on the cheek and said, 'Thanks for the ride' (I may be rubbish at burlesque but I'm great at innuendo), that I'd hear from him again. The internet makes hunting people down remarkably easy, and I have never been difficult to find. I was confident that I'd given him enough information about myself that, if he wanted to, he could get in touch with me. And I got the feeling he wanted to.

The obvious bonus was that, by saying goodbye, by shutting the car door without a second glance, I could tell myself, and my friends (and my sister, importantly), that it was my version of a zipless fuck. It meant nothing; it was a rebound; I just wanted to prove to myself that I was still attractive, that I could still find a man who wanted to be with me, even if it was just for one night, in his childhood bed.

It was three days before I heard from him – a message sent through Facebook (like I said, I've never been hard to track down). He told me he'd really enjoyed meeting me. 'I think it's pretty rare to find a girl who likes *Star Wars*!' I didn't know whether to laugh or cry; the predictability of men never ceases to show its true colours. He told me he was away the following weekend, 'going to Amsterdam with the guys', but asked if I'd have dinner with him the following week.

I said yes, of course – I hadn't been asked on a dinner date in weeks, maybe months. I didn't think Irish men knew that dinner dates were a *thing*; I felt as though no one wanted to invest in dinner until they were sure they had any serious interest in the other person. Drinks were casual, while dinner was a commitment, the dating form of kryptonite for the straight male.

We texted that weekend, while he was away. It

was raining in Amsterdam, he told me. They'd rented bikes and got soaked, and his friends had booked the entire group into a cheap hostel, with shared rooms and communal bathrooms. He'd had to sleep on the top bunk; in the middle of the night, he'd been woken up by the obnoxiously loud farting of the man in the bunk below.

This was a good sign, I thought. Though I was known to emit the odd loud fart of my own, I was also strongly against vacationing in youth hostels and I would rather die than cycle around a foreign city in the rain. One has to have standards – it was comforting to me that ours appeared, at least on this micro-level, to be shared.

Scott checked in a few days before our planned date, to see if I was 'still on'. Would I like to go to this newly opened bar-restaurant in the city centre – he'd heard it was good.

I said yes (of course). I'd been to the venue before, but only for a PR event, which never allows you to judge the calibre of a location. At press launches, only the best will do – the best Prosecco, the most popular canapés. Staff are sent in, early in the morning, to give the room the best clean of its life. While the average, paying customer may not notice mismatched wine glasses or the beer-stained carpet beneath their feet, brands paying top dollar will – not to mention the fact that there appears to be a belief among PR and marketing professionals that the more you spoil a journalist, the more they will feel indebted to you, and, ergo, inclined to write positive things about the brand in question. It's a tangled web.

It was a different vibe, that night, on our first date. I had walked in from my house, on that cool October night, in skinny jeans, a black top, a leather jacket (reliable first-date costumery) and ankle boots that were high enough to qualify as heels and low enough to allow for a fifteen-minute walk.

He met me outside. I remember smiling, removing my earphones, greeting him with a hug, a brief kiss on the cheek, close enough to his mouth to remind us both that this was not merely a friendly outing. He was taller than I remembered, and better-looking. He had gorgeous, kind eyes and a big smile – he immediately made me feel comfortable, safe and relaxed. *Uh-oh*, I thought. *There goes my zipless fuck.*

Scott had booked a table; he opened the door and ushered me in ahead of him; when it came time to pay the bill, he did it surreptitiously, while I was in the bathroom. I was impressed. This was not the kind of gallantry I was used to, and though my feminism would have me argue against door-opening and bill-paying and ladies-firsting, the part of me that had always loved a happily ever after was not-so-secretly delighted that, finally, it felt like I was getting mine.

After dinner, we went to a bar by the Liffey, the river that bisects the city, dividing it from north to south. The bar was owned by the same group that owned the restaurant, the same group that would, in the following five years, while we fell in love – and out again – swallow up every vacant property Dublin had to offer and erect boutique hotels and bourgeois cinemas and vintage-style diners, until the entire city had an eerie Edward Scissorhands quality about it, as if every notable venue had been designed by the same person, someone with a penchant for olde worlde lamps and exaggerated typography (and neon).

I drank overpriced G&Ts and insisted on paying; I had remembered my women's libbing by then and didn't want to feel like I was being bought. Because I was still living with Liam – and now realised that Scott was not living with his mum in a cool, modern, sexually liberated way – we were confined to this one night, to these drinks in this bar.

We sat upstairs on a black pleather sofa – easier to wipe clean, which is a thought that grosses me out in the harsh light of day, but something I entirely forget when it's dark and I'm three sheets to the wind – by the DJ box and watched a group of twentysome-things dancing enthusiastically to Calvin Harris's 'Acceptable in the 80s'.

When I moved to kiss him, Scott expressed sur-prise; he hadn't thought I was that into him, hadn't thought I was that into *this*. This is not an isolated incident – I have had more than one man, on the first or second date, tell me that he wasn't sure of my feel-ings, that he'd thought I was 'not that into' him. It's an ambiguity I am not aware of and which, in any case, seems to dissipate quickly.

A few dates in, there is no way anyone could mis-take my open enthusiasm for anything else. I'm only short of scrawling our names, combined, in a diary, using some complicated mathematical equation to work out the percentage likelihood of our love match based on the letters that make up our names. I might start out defensive and slightly bitchy, but it doesn't take much for me to go full steam in the opposite direction.

I waited for Liam to move out before inviting Scott over – what had been a 'no rush' scenario became my daily bugbear. I would quiz Liam, hourly, as to whether he'd seen any suitable housing ads; I would offer to drive him to see them, to send emails or make calls on his behalf.

If you were to tell this story to me now about someone who had dated my best friend and was treating him this way, pushing him out of their shared home, despite having declared, mere weeks earlier, that they would, of course, remain friends, I would be furious. I am furious, at myself, at the self who replaced Liam so quickly and made it so very clear to him that he was replaceable. But, as with most of my friendships, I have more pressing apologies to make than this one.

We 'made it official' about two months in; Scott told me his friends had been asking about our relationship status, but it was clear that it was he who wanted to know. I, too, wanted to firm things up, to use terrible corporate-speak, but I didn't want to be the one to do it. I had too much riding on this construction I'd been working on, this idea I'd been propagating of me as a relaxed, laid-back, non-monogamy-seeking singleton.

I'd even gone on two dates with another man I'd met on Tinder. He was quiet and softly spoken, from 'the country', as my mother would say, although, being from the great city of Cork, he would probably reject that categorisation. We'd gone for drinks in two different pubs, on two different nights, where he'd made little to no eye contact and then kissed me suddenly and aggressively on the street outside on the way home. He was a good kisser, but he kept his hands exactly on my hips, pressing the heel of his palm on my hip bones in a way that made me uncomfortable, although I couldn't quite tell why.

Once Scott had clarified our relationship status, I texted this man and told him I'd met someone and it was getting serious. A few years later, I saw him in the cinema with a male friend, and I wondered if he was still single, if he still hated living in Dublin or if he had met someone, settled down, put down roots. I've always been incredibly curious about the lives of people who almost-but-not-quite became a part of mine.

It might sound idyllic, the beginnings of this relationship, but it was fraught with insecurities (mine) and what I perceived as a kind of emotional numbness (his). In therapy, a few years in, my psychologist would ask me if I felt that he met my emotional needs and I would have to tell her no, he didn't, but that I didn't think it was possible to get all of one's needs met in the one go. Sometimes we make sacrifices, find the things we need in a variety of places. Life is like a buffet; we have to choose from an array of dishes before we are fully satisfied. (As analogies go, this is especially fallacious for someone like me, who hates buffets, and just wants to eat a regular dinner – with the result that I only ever choose one or two things from the selection laid out in front of me, and do not relish the process.)

In the early days of our relationship, I would quiz Scott, over and over again, as to whether he actually *wanted* to be with me. He was always very casual, almost nonchalant, about us seeing one another. He cancelled on me several times, giving very reasonable excuses: the train wasn't running, there were no buses, his car had broken down. Each time it happened, I would think to myself, surely if he *really* wanted to see me ... Love finds a way.

We had been together for about three months when I invited him to come to Mass, one Sunday, to hear the choir of which I was a member sing gospel tunes at regular intervals between homilies and gospels and communion and signs of peace. He said he would come, but didn't – the train, or the bus, or the car, let him down again.

The following day, I told him it was clear to me that this was going nowhere, that he was no longer interested in whatever it was he had thought I had to offer. He protested, told me that wasn't true and then, seeming resigned, said, 'Okay, will you meet me for coffee after work?'

I think about this moment, sometimes, about what would have happened if I'd insisted on leaving things there, if I'd walked away at this first early sign of indifference. Where would we be now?

Of course, I wasn't really trying to initiate a breakup. I can count on one hand the number of breakups I've initiated and actually meant it. This was my attempt to push him to prove that he was serious about me. By pushing him away, I would force him to *find a way* to keep us together.

I walked down to meet him after work that day and he kissed me on the mouth, as he had any other time we'd seen one another, then asked where we were going for dinner. I was taken aback, and I told him as much. 'We're breaking up,' I told him. 'No, we're not,' he replied.

We went for dinner; he stayed in my house that night. It wasn't the last time I would suggest that we break up, but it was the last time I thought it might actually happen. His casual insistence that this was not a possibility had, as it turns out, been enough to reassure me that he didn't want to break up. I was convinced that he wanted a girlfriend, that he wanted to be in this relationship, going on these dates, having these weekend-morning cuddles; I just wasn't altogether convinced that he wanted to do it all with me. Still, I chose to be optimistic.

When I told Scott that I loved him, six months in, he said nothing. When I got upset – I mean, I know we shouldn't say 'I love you' specifically to hear it back, but we do, don't we? – he told me that he wasn't sure he would ever fall in love. He didn't know that he would ever feel that way about anyone, he said, and he wasn't sure why.

I was angry at what I perceived to be his sheer ego.

'You're not a special snowflake,' I told him (I mean, who *wouldn't* love me?). 'You're not some anomaly, a robot human who's incapable of feeling human emotions.' Of course, you don't need to be a robot to have different and unique ways of relating to others, and of understanding and experiencing your own emotions. Humans are not homogeneous, although a lot of what we read and consume would have us believe they are. Emotional intelligence is not, as my therapist would tell me time and again, one-size-fits-all.

The same friends – the friends who had served as wingmen for him to interrupt my burlesque show, the friends who would take him to Amsterdam on 'the worst holiday' of his life, the friends who would go out with him on a Friday night and drink copious drinks ('maybe eight pints and some shots') and encourage him to call me at 3 a.m. and leave me long, incoherent voicemails – would prove to be instrumental in the progression (or lack thereof) of our relationship.

It wasn't so much that they didn't approve of me, per se, but they were all so much younger than I was, so that when I suggested doing things that made sense to me, like moving in together (after a year), or going on a holiday together (after eighteen months), he would tell me that it was too soon.

'None of my friends are living with their girlfriends,' he would say, as if I particularly cared what his mates were doing with their lives.

'Well, my friends are all living with their boyfriends,'

I would tell him. 'Some of them are engaged, one of them has a baby – should I be trying to live my life on exactly the same timeline as them?'

He agreed that no, I shouldn't, but still: he moved in with a school friend after we'd been dating for a year. His apartment was just twenty minutes' walk away from mine, to be fair, but it was very much a bachelor pad, decorated in navy and grey and stocked with cans of beer and an array of PlayStation games.

That summer, he would pull out of accompanying me to a friend's wedding in Spain because he was studying for his finance exams; two months later, he would announce, with a week to go, that he couldn't go to another friend's wedding, an hour away from home, because his exams were coming up soon and he was too stressed. I didn't realise it at the time, but I think it was the marriage itself he didn't want to witness; it was as if he was in denial about the lives my friends were making for themselves, in denial about the life I might soon want.

We'd been dating for two years when he told me he'd booked a three-week holiday to Southeast Asia with 'the lads', to visit a friend who was living in South Korea, then travel through China and home via Dubai.

Our relationship existed as a kind of semi-autonomous state, entirely aside from his life with his friends and his family and his career. It was only after we'd been dating for four years that I went on the occasional night out with his friends, all of whom had known one another since high school and spoke exclusively in in-jokes that I could never hope to understand.

It sounds like there were warning signs dropping like bombs across the landscape of our love story, but our relationship was, in plenty of ways, really good. We enjoyed a lot of the same things – we loved trying new restaurants and going to see new movies the minute they came out, and eventually we would join a weightlifting gym and go together, early in the morning before work, to encourage each other and, more often than that, laugh at one another's ugly lifting faces.

We laughed a lot.

He told me he loved me one evening in a hotel in Galway. We had gone for a minibreak, booking a king-sized room overlooking Galway Bay, heading out for dinner in the local seafood bar and eating very good food before retiring to our room with a bottle of wine, I think, to watch Eurovision.

I have always been a big fan of Eurovision, even since what a lot of Irish people would term 'the shift', when it became less about the song and more about the performance. Honestly, I don't particularly care how great the songwriting is; I'm not there for the melody, or even for the singer. I'm there for the flag-waving and the glitter and the glamour and the sheer mania of waiting to see who will get *douze points* and who, chillingly, will get *nul points*. I'm clearly not a good sport, because I also really enjoy the fact that the British jury almost always gives us *douze points* while we, still bitter from centuries of colonisation, refuse to give them a single one. Sometimes it's the little things that warm the heart.

About three years into our relationship, I asked what he thought about the next step. We'd talked about it, on and off – I am incredibly judgemental about people who claim never to have spoken about marriage, or babies, or 'next steps', with their partners – but I wanted to get some answers, rather than relying on vague assurances of future commitments.

I wanted to get married; I thought I maybe wanted babies, despite having been convinced, until then, that I didn't. He said he was certain he didn't, but I thought – maybe condescendingly – that he was just young, that he would change his mind, or at least begin to, as I had. Our age discrepancy meant that he didn't quite get to put things off, at least not when it came to a biological clock that was not exactly ticking in my favour, but he was not in any rush to make a promise either way.

He did tell me, then, that he thought we would probably get engaged the following year – we could get married the year after. Either way, he said, he wanted to spend the rest of his life with me.

I had no reason not to believe him.

When, a year later, I brought it up again, he seemed shocked. Had it really been a year? He still felt too young. None of his friends were engaged, or married (when one of them would become engaged, three months later, it wouldn't matter; by then we were too close to the end to go back) and he had a lot he wanted to do first – what about buying a house instead, he suggested?

But we were nowhere near that – or, at least, I wasn't. I have never been good with money, and by that I mean that I have never cared about money.

Money is a means to an end – and the end is consumption, or enjoyment of life, or time spent with friends. I have never had enough savings to buy a small car, say, or even an expensive handbag. Any over-the-top purchases I've ever made have been on credit.

It would be remiss of me not to acknowledge my part in this slow, steady disintegration. I was, for at least half of the time that we were together – two and a half years out of five, or 912-odd days out of 1,825 – suffering from a depression that had been diagnosed but was not quite yet being managed. I was on and off medication, in and out of therapy – it would be three years into our relationship before I would find a therapist I thought really understood me, and could help me move forward to a better place, where my mental health was concerned.

He was there as I cried in bed, unable to see a way to get up, to get dressed, to get out of the house and do the things I had to do to keep my life going: go to work, speak to friends, *get on with it*. At the time, I was frustrated by his inability to be there for me in the kind of way I wanted him to be.

I wanted him to hold me, to lie under the covers and tell me it would be okay. Instead, he was up and dressed, gently encouraging me to get up and dressed, too, telling me that things would feel better once I was up and breathing some fresh air. 'Would you go for a walk?' My therapist suggested to me, more than once, that we had different ways of communicating our emotions – and that perhaps our incompatibility on that front wasn't as much a problem to be solved as it was a reality to be accepted.

In hindsight, while I believe that old dogs probably *can* learn new tricks, if they want to, I'm not sure they should have to, especially not to fulfil the needs and expectations of someone else. I spent far too much time and energy, back then, feeling angry at Scott's apparent unwillingness to change for me – and being openly angry and frustrated at his seeming inability to try. It wasn't fair to him; he had shown me, from the very first moment, who he was, but I had chosen to think that he was wrong, that he didn't even know the first thing about himself. (I was, after all, older – and wiser – than he was.)

We spent a lot of our lives together expecting one another to change, I think. I was waiting for him to grow up, a fact I shared with him far too frequently, and he was waiting for . . . what, I'm not sure. Maybe he was waiting for me to get better, to be 'cured' of the depression that was the source of all of my problems (my general lethargy, my never wanting to go out and get drunk, spending all of my money to try to feed some insatiable hunger for some kind of happiness that seemed to come in an online order). I've never asked him.

The final six months of our relationship were a hellscape I wish never to repeat. Sure, they had nice moments – where we would connect over dinner or lunch, or on a rare night out together – but they also contained too many moments of pain, of heartbreak, to count.

He went out a lot, either with his friends or with his workmates. He was younger than me, I told myself, but the bigger truth was that he was a far more social animal than I was, and he loved to drink, to be drunk, to revel in the confidence gained from a feed of pints. He didn't mind spending the following day in a hung-over haze, while I couldn't face it. I was depressed enough already – to add a chemically induced black cloud to the mix would seem to ensure an unmitigated disaster.

The night it all fell apart – although that's not quite fair, because it was cracked before that night, but this was the final chink, the ultimate destruction of the property I had considered ours – I was in the kitchen, listening to Janelle Monáe's new song, 'Make Me Feel'. I wasn't especially depressed on that night, I don't think – but I was in my PJs, which was the default outfit I would shimmy into the moment I got in from work. One doesn't have to be despondent to want to feel comfortable, is my attitude.

It was past midnight, but not late enough for me to expect him home – so when he walked in the door I thought he was giving a repeat performance of that first New Year's Eve we spent apart, when I stayed in and he went out, and he came home before 1 a.m., telling me that he'd missed me, that he hadn't enjoyed his night without me, that he should have spent it with me. I thought that this night, this moment, was one of those moments. (It was not.)

'I kissed someone.'

It came out fast, as if he'd been running and couldn't wait to impart some crucial information. He was the messenger. This was the message – and it couldn't wait.

It was so improbable to me that I didn't believe him, and then, after another look at his face, flushed, sweating, impossibly anguished (finally! Some emotion!), I did. I kept asking, 'What?!' as if I couldn't hear him, or didn't understand the words he was saying, but I could and did – I just didn't want to.

He told me he was sorry. It hadn't meant anything. They'd been dancing – he and this nameless, faceless girl, a girl whose face I would look for in every twentysomething woman I saw in the following weeks and months – and it had 'just happened'. For what it's worth, I don't believe things just happen. I believe we make decisions and then we make other decisions and whatever happens, ultimately, is a consequence of those decisions, combined.

Scott asked, then, if I wanted him to leave. Should he go home, to his mother's house, the house they had 'shared', on that very first night that we met? I said yes – but what I really meant was, you've hurt me. You've done something very, very wrong and you need to know that, but I love you and I need you to prove to me that you love me too and maybe, just maybe, this is the perfect opportunity for you to do this. I immediately began to write the story of our relationship in my head and to incorporate this 'blip', this pothole that had tripped us up and would, in the end, become an anecdote about couples who make it, despite what seemed like impossible odds.

He went home and I stayed in the house (our house) and cried and cuddled my dog (our dog) and worried about what would happen next. He texted me to say he was sorry; he texted me to say he was home; he texted me to say he'd call me the following day. I told him not to – I told him I needed some time.

I am amazed that I managed to make it through this charade in any kind of convincing way (I have never asked him if he was convinced, mind you), but it all began to fall apart pretty quickly, and by midweek I was begging him to come home and writing him long, beseeching emails. I wrote this email and kept it in my drafts for about twenty minutes before calling him on the phone and – for some inexplicable, agonising reason – reading it out loud to him and saying, 'You don't have to respond right away.' (There is no age limit on dramatic emo behaviour.)

We broke up today. Kind of. We're taking some time to figure it out. Or you are. I feel like I have it figured out. I love you. We're in love. Or I am. I'm not sure any more.

They teach us in fairy tales that love will conquer all. They teach us in pop music that all you need is love. They teach us in literature that a single man in possession of a good fortune must be in want of a wife. But the reality is some weird amalgamation of all, and none, of the above. Sometimes love will not conquer financial strain. Sometimes all you need is love and a few shared interests. Sometimes a single man is neither in possession of a good fortune nor in want of a wife.

I miss you already, so much that my heart hurts.

I swear I got thinner today, despite the fact that my appetite has gone nowhere (more's the pity; the one silver lining that we are promised with a broken heart is a reduced appetite and, ergo, a reduction in mass. Chance would be a fine thing). I bought a pack of cigarettes and smoked four, then threw the pack in the bin. I took it out an hour later, smoked another. It's back in the bin now but it cost me €12 so I think I might take it away. Would you throw €10 away? I think not.

I think we can get through this because I love you, and you me. I do believe that, despite my saying that I wasn't sure you loved me as much as my friend Ciara's husband loves her. I see the way he looks at her from across the room. But maybe I just never catch the glances you give me when I'm not looking – isn't that the point? Maybe I just don't know you're giving them.

There is so much about our relationship that is good and fun and loving. We care about each other deeply. We laugh together. You let me warm up my feet in the space between your legs at night, when we're readying ourselves for bed. You make me endless cups of tea even though I never drink the whole thing. I remind you to call your mother and I make homemade granola with extra raisins, even though I think they add a bitter tang that ruins the whole batch. We do things for each other.

I know that lately we've kept coming around to the question of whether we should break up. Things are difficult; should we break up? We're stressed about money; should we break up? We don't know where our relationship is going; should we break up? In hindsight I feel like we've been answering a question with a question. Why are things difficult? How can we sort out our money issues? Should we make some plans for our relationship? 'Let's break up' is not the answer to any of those questions.

Right now it feels like I'm waiting for you. For you to change your mind and realise that you love me so much that breaking up is not an option. But I need to recapture the flag. I need to think about myself, too. I've spent such a long time wondering if you love me and wanting you to show that love and wondering if you love me enough, that I haven't spent any time asking myself what I want. Is this what I want?

I think it is. I think you are. I think we just work. Love is not an easy thing to find and I found it with you. I don't want to throw it away.

He came back, of course; I don't think he quite had the courage to end things then, on that sour note. I think that would have made him too much of the bad guy and, in a way, given me a get-out-of-jail-free card that, to his mind, I did not deserve.

The problem is, as soon as one person cheats, the other person is automatically designated as the victim. Once you have done the ultimate wrong thing, there is nothing for your partner to be but right. You are the devil; they are the angel. I was the soul of benevolence and virtue; he was a foil to my open-hearted, forthright love and affection.

In my mind and, I think, in his, the onus was on Scott, now, to earn back the trust that I had previously given him so blindly. It should have been clear to me, and to him, when he didn't make that effort, that some part of him saw this as an opportunity to close a chapter that had been slowly coming to its conclusion, whether or not either of us was quite prepared for it.

Instead, we spent another month together, making love tearily (on my part, anyway) and going on dates and making an array of superficial 'efforts' that amounted to not very much at all. I was still changing into my PJs the minute I got home from work and planning to go to the cinema then cancelling at the last minute because I just wasn't 'feeling great'. I was still too unwell to go on nights out; I had no interest in drinking, really, or even in going to the bars he drank in, which seemed to be populated by women in body-con dresses who would, through no fault of their own, make me feel old and frumpy and unattractive.

We had gone out together once, two years in, with

a group of his friends. The girls all wore sexy mini-dresses and spoke exclusively to one another while the boys talked about football and made jokes about girls (of course). I had worn a sparkly dress and a pair of leopard-print heels, and one of his male friends, drunk and over-excited, had gone around the room pointing out how 'funky' they were, like he was witnessing his mother go on her first girls' night out since the divorce.

And, despite saying that he wanted to stay together, that he still saw us spending our lives together, that he wanted to move forward together . . . Scott didn't see us getting engaged 'any time soon'.

He went out twice, sometimes three times, a week with his friends, or his workmates. He would come home at two or three in the morning, barely able to walk. I would wake up as he stumbled up the stairs, fumbling for the light or the door – once, I had to leap out of bed and steer him out of our guest bedroom and into the bathroom, in the nick of time. 'I'm *going* to the *bathroom*!' he told me, indignantly.

On the last night we would ever spend together, Scott was out for drinks 'with work'. He had stopped telling me what time he'd be home; a recurring argument we'd have would be due to his saying he'd be home at one time and then coming in four hours later, not having updated me or responded to any of my texts.

I had texted him at around 10 p.m. to ask how things were going, but he hadn't responded. That was fine, I thought; it was fine, I'm cool (why do we spend so much time trying to be cool about things that do not deserve to be met with laid-back cool-girl energy?), it's cool. When he finally rolled in, it was after 3 a.m. and he could barely talk. I said hello and he grunted a reply to me. When I asked how his night was, he ignored me (it's cool, I'm cool).

He got into bed and turned over so I was facing his back. I did the same, but noticed the tell-tale blue light of his mobile phone, the signature small movements that signified the composition of furious texts (either that or he was writing down the story of his night). I asked who he was texting; no one, he said, just Carrie, a friend from work. He put the phone down.

I was not hurt any more – I think I'd given him all the hurt feelings he would be getting by then – but I was raging. My palms were sweaty, my face burning, heart racing. I had never truly understood people whose rage gives rise to impulsive violence, until that moment.

When he fell asleep, breathing the deep breaths of the utterly sozzled, I slipped out of bed – unnecessarily delicately for someone next to an inebriated man, honestly – and read through their texts.

They were the kind of innocent, yet suggestive, messages sent between two people who hadn't quite acknowledged the fact that theirs was a mutual crush. Carrie hoped he got home safely (we did live on the 'bad' side of town, to be fair); he said he was afraid for his life; she told him to call her if he needed to be saved. (From a totally objective point of view, I was oddly impressed with the way he accepted this gender-role reversal – he could never be accused of being in possession of the type of fragile male ego seen in many others of his sex.)

I scrolled back further, to their first exchange. 'Hey, it's Scott from work. Is that Eurovision party still on?' My blood began to cool in my veins as I realised that this was the very same Eurovision party he had gone to, earlier in the year, without me. It had been held in a colleague's very small flat, he said; it was for work people only.

Her response to him: 'Yep! From 8 p.m. – bring friends / whoever!' She had not said the word 'girl-friend', which made me wonder if she even knew about me – but she had said to bring friends. She had said to bring 'whoever', in fact, which he had taken to mean, 'bring no one – it's only for workmates and anyway, my apartment is too small for extras.'

I knew, right then, as I placed his phone back on his side of the bed, that it was over – but I also knew that he was in no state to receive this information. So I waited.

I didn't go back to sleep. I was too angry, full of adrenaline and plotting the speech that I would give to mark the cessation of this period of our lives, the dissolution of our relationship. So I waited.

I sat on the bed next to him, my rage growing with each and every drunken breath he took. I finally woke him at dawn, shaking him roughly and saying, 'Scott. We need to talk.' He looked more alarmed than I'd ever seen him, as alarmed as I could imagine he'd be if he were waking up to a roaring fire, burning its way through the house.

Despite my three-hour wait, the build-up in my mind as I planned exactly what I'd say to him and what he would say back (please, no, I love you, don't, don't do this), it happened with very little fanfare. I told him I thought we should break up; I recounted the events of the previous night, when he got home and texted his 'friend', the Eurovision-related betrayal I had unearthed when I searched through his phone.

He objected to my reasoning – there was nothing going on between them, he told me, they were just friends – but he didn't argue with me. It was very calm. In one final attempt to elicit some dramatic reaction, I told him that, in the future, when he told the story of how we'd broken up, he needed to know that this was all. His. Fault. He was the one who'd stopped trying; he was the one who'd cheated on me, then made no effort to make it up to me; he was the one who continued to go out, get drunk and live a life totally aside from the life we shared with one another. He wasn't sure he agreed, but that was fine – it was fine. He was sorry.

He went home, then, one final time, to the house he now shared, once again, with his mother. He continued paying rent for the following two months; he didn't want me to have to worry about anything. He didn't want to leave me in the lurch.

When he came over to pick up his things a week later, we hugged in the hallway as we said goodbye. He patted my bum in a familiar gesture he'd adopted at some stage I couldn't quite pinpoint. 'You can't do that any more,' I told him. He had the good grace to look slightly sheepish.

We'd meet up again a couple of times over the ensuing months. Each time, I would wonder if this would be the day he'd tell me how much he missed me, declare that he couldn't live without me, beg me to get back with him. At the same time, I knew it was over. I knew that we had spent too long waiting for the other to change, to adapt. It was clear that we were both capable of change, just not in the direction that was required.

Three months after our breakup, he revealed that he and Carrie had kissed on a night out. It 'just happened', he said. Within another month, they made it 'official'; a year later, they moved in together in San Francisco. A year after that, they were, he told me, talking about marriage, 'for Green Card purposes', he said, but this made no sense as neither of them had a Green Card at the time; they were there on non-immigrant working visas, so marrying one another would offer no advantage. I wasn't sure if it was a deliberate lie, or just a mistake on his part.

I suppose it doesn't matter, but I did cringe, slightly, at the idea that he might be trying to spare my feelings, that he would be trying to make me feel better about the fact that he was happy to marry her, after two years, when he didn't want to marry me, after five.

We still text, occasionally. I'm not sure if it would be possible for me to share a life with someone for that long (1,825 days) without feeling in some way bound to them, without maintaining a curiosity about their life, the goings-on within it. He enquires about my nephews; I ask how his mum is. There is a lot of love there, I think.

Though I have – more than once – wished that he would act like he wanted me back, that he would tell me that I was the love of his life, that he would make me feel as if I am *wanted* by him, I have never thought to myself, *We really should have stayed together*. Because we shouldn't have. He was not the one for me – and I was not the one for him.

I have been happier in the years since we broke up than I was in the years before. I think, sometimes, that humans are more intuitive than we give ourselves credit for. I think we both felt a certain want from the other; he knew that I wanted him to be more of this and less of that, and I knew that he, too, wanted some things from me that I was not willing or able to give. As a result, we made one another feel like we weren't enough.

I'm not quite good enough, in the Biblical sense of being 'good', meaning selfless and well-meaning and kind, to hope that he and Carrie are happy together. He texted me one Christmas and told me they were in South America for the holidays, and that she had contracted food poisoning and he was looking after her. I just thought, *There but for the grace of God . . .*

Johnny

He stood me up on our second date.

I had bought tickets, months beforehand, for a showing of *The Princess Bride* in Dublin's newest bougie cinema, the one with the velvet couches and the table service and the chicken tenders that came with just the right amount of sweet paprika.

They weren't cheap tickets, although the money wasn't – isn't ever, really – the point.

We had arranged to meet that morning on O'Connell Street, to take the bus together to the cinema. I had checked the bus times, firmed up the logistics.

Even if we missed the first bus, the second would get us there on time, so I didn't panic when he was five minutes late, nor ten, having yet to respond to either of my texts. It's hard to compose a text to a second date, asking if they're on their way, because you're so busy – *I* was so busy – trying to appear nonchalant and as if timekeeping and plans and schedules aren't all that important to you. I imagine I said something like, 'Hey – everything okay?!' when

203

what I really wanted to say was, 'Are you still coming? Because, if not, I'll go on my own.'

By the time he finally responded, the second bus was due any minute. 'Shit! I didn't hear my alarm!' he wrote. 'Are you joking?' I asked. I was sure he was joking. 'No! You should have called me!' he replied. It was subtle, but it was the first of many instances in which he would blame me for his mistakes. I should have known; I should have called; I should have calmed down; I should have understood.

I didn't write back immediately. As I stood there composing my brief responses to him – feeling irritated by this flagrant disregard for my time, my plans, my preferences – the second bus went by. I thought about getting a taxi, but realised that would just add a further expense to the endeavour – I would sit through my favourite film in a blind rage, and the entire ordeal would end up costing me more than €50.

I stood still for a minute, imagining the *Sliding Doors* version of the day, where he'd showed up on time – maybe he'd brought flowers! – and we were now making ourselves comfortable in our plush sofa seats, sipping fizzy drinks from real glasses, smiling at one another in the dim lamplight.

Another text.

'C'mere, I'll come into town anyway,' he said, as if he was doing me a favour. 'We'll hang out, we'll have a nice day.'

I wasn't convinced. 'It doesn't matter,' I said. 'Forget about it.'

'No,' he said, firmly. 'I'm on my way in now, we'll do something nice.'

I gave in. People make mistakes, I thought, and decided not to go home, wandering into the shops for a browse while I waited for him to arrive.

Another text. 'Before I get on this bus, are you gonna be in a mood with me now?'

We had met – and I don't mean this to sound like an excuse, so much as it should sound like a reason – at a particularly low point in my life. My relationship of five years with Scott had ended a few weeks previously and I felt lost, lonely and a bit panicked, worried that, at thirty-three, I had left it too late to meet someone else.

It was, of course, too soon to enter into any new romance, to expose myself to the rollercoaster of online dating, but I needed to know that there were men out there who would see photographs of me, read the details I had chosen to share on my profile, and feel *something*, some stirring of romance or sexual attraction, or both.

It wasn't *just* that I was single, for the first time in five years, at an age that felt too old to be single, to be starting over, to be investing time in something that may end up as nothing at all – but I had also been going through a sort of career crisis that had left me all at sea, unsure of what I wanted to do or, even, who I was.

I had left my career as a journalist and social influencer and qualified as a personal trainer, having been the target of some online harassment that had, terrifyingly, gone offline, when someone tied helium balloons to the door of the house I lived in.

The balloons were covered in a kind of primary-school scrawl calling me names, insulting my looks, pointing out my high opinion of myself. I wanted to install CCTV cameras but Scott had, at the time, said that I was overreacting, which, in hindsight? *Fuck him*. When a man tells you that you're overreacting, he's just short of calling you hysterical and having you committed to a sanatorium for women with wandering wombs.

I worked as a personal trainer for almost a year, enjoying the face-to-face interactions that differentiated it from the face-to-laptop career I had been so used to. But the money was *terrible* – I think the most I made in a single month was €1,450, despite the fact that, by personal training standards, I was relatively busy – and the hours were miserable, and I was also spending far too much time worrying about my own body, which was being written about online as 'hardly the body of a personal trainer!' You can take the influencer out of the online sphere, but you can't make people stop talking about her, apparently.

By the time I met Johnny, I was starting over *again*, tail between my legs, reverting to blogging about my day-to-day and considering what kind of sponsored content would fit in with my former-fitness-maven vibe. In one of our first conversations, he told me he knew of me, that he'd thought I might, in fact, have been catfishing Rosemary Mac Cabe.

Johnny

The truth? I was delighted. I've always wanted someone to catfish me. It strikes me as a supreme humble brag to moan about people using your photographs to lure romantic interests on dating apps.

I was less flattered, mind you, when he told me he could help to rehabilitate my image. 'You need an online makeover,' he'd said in one of our very early conversations. 'People really *hate* you!' He laughed as he said the words, not *un*kindly, but saying something unkind in a kind way doesn't negate the fact that it's a shitty thing to say in the first place, does it?!

It didn't occur to me, at the time, that this was a sort of PR-focused negging. *You need me*, he was saying. *I can improve you.*

As for him, I remember the first few days of exchanging messages – at first, within the apparatus of Tinder and, later, on WhatsApp. He told me about his struggles with addiction, an addiction that had taken hold while he worked at a job he hated, with a boss who also hated him and was, at least, according to him, not afraid to show it in various ways that violated every employment law going. He told me that he would drink a shoulder of vodka right after he signed off his twelve-hour shift, and another when he got home – the aim was to get drunk enough during his time off work in order to forget he'd soon have to go back.

He shared details of his mental health struggles: he'd suffered from depression and anxiety since losing that job, and attended a weekly support meeting for his alcoholism – not AA, which he felt was too steeped in religion and morality for him – and saw a therapist to discuss his mental illness. I loved his ability to be vulnerable, to talk about feelings as things that could apply to him as much as they could apply to me, and to work on himself, to want to be – and do – better.

Bear in mind that my ex – a man I'd spent five years dating, and had lived with for three – had once told me that he didn't know if he ever *would* fall in love with me. He wasn't sure that love was an emotion he was capable of feeling. If he was ever sad, or angry, or confused, or frustrated, he kept it to himself. At the time, his stoicism had felt a lot like distance, as though he had put a wall up between us and was determined that it should not be compromised. Johnny, on the other hand, was happily talking about his feelings via text, which was refreshing.

I was in Cologne with my mum on a weekend away – a weekend that was meant to be happening with Scott, for whom my mum ended up being a far more entertaining stand-in – when our initial flirtation began to turn into something more. 'I feel like I have a crush,' he told me, coquettishly, and I resisted the urge to ask, 'A crush on me?!' It seemed obvious but really, I wasn't quite sure.

For our first date, he came over to my house and we took the dog to the park. Whatever reluctance I had about meeting a man I didn't know at my home was quickly squashed when he told me, laughingly, 'It's not like I don't know where you live.' (Why are red flags always so much more vivid in hindsight?)

Johnny

A dog walk seemed like a nice first-date idea. If nothing else, we would have the dog to distract us. An awkward silence could be dispelled by calling the dog, throwing a ball, making her do a trick – by that I mean, come back when called, the only trick she'd ever learned.

He turned up to my front door in a black T-shirt and black shorts, Converse high-tops, carrying a backpack. His passion was photography, and he took his camera everywhere; I guess you never know when you might stumble across the perfect photograph. He would later take several beautiful photographs of my dog, one of which I have hung in my living room. I don't think of him when I look at it – just of her, her big brown eyes, those bushy eyebrows. He would only ever take one of me, shot from below, as I came down an elevator. When he looked at it later, he said, 'Ugh. I cropped out the hands – you should never crop out the hands.'

The local park we walked in that first day was one I often took my dog to. We knew people there, in the way a dog owner will know the names of other people's dogs, if not those of their owners. We met a man I knew to say hello to, with his three dogs – an old golden retriever and two little mutts – and he stopped to talk to us as our dogs did the kind of rough and tumble dogs seem to enjoy.

The dogs' owner chatted to us in an unselfconscious way, which served to highlight just how self-conscious I felt. He asked questions of us as one might ask questions of a couple, a duo you expect to answer as one entity, knowing almost everything about each other. I had known Johnny, and only by text, for a fortnight; I was still surprised by the look of him – shorter than I'd imagined, and somehow stockier, *bigger*, too.

Later, Johnny would laugh as he told me he wasn't sure we'd ever get away from the man in the park, and I was impressed with – rather than concerned by – how he'd been able to be so charming to this man he clearly hadn't wanted to talk to. 'His dogs *stank*!' he exclaimed. He was a big fan of hand-washing, now that I think of it, even in those heady, pre-Covid days where we all hugged one another, willy-nilly. That was the first time he'd tell me to wash my hands – but not, of course, the last.

I introduced him to Clare – my housemate, but also my oldest friend, and probably one of the most important people in my life – that evening, in our living room. He didn't stand up off the couch, just inclined his head and said 'hi' before turning back to the television. She would think him rude and a bit unfriendly; later, he would tell me that he had farted mere seconds before we walked into the room and was trying to stay as still as possible so as not to disperse the aroma.

We went up to my bedroom soon afterwards, lay down on the bed and talked. I leaned up on one elbow, wondering if we were ever going to kiss; when we finally did, he heralded the moment with a 'for God's *sake* would you come here!' as if he had been trying to kiss me for *ages*, as if I had been ignoring his signals, talking too much while he tried to romance me. I felt like a child, chastised for speaking out of place, but I was also delighted by the insinuation that he'd been dying to kiss me as much as I had him.

We kissed for ages, the way you kiss someone you're kissing for the first time, someone who, in that moment, you imagine you might want to kiss for the rest of your life. He was a great kisser; he took deep breaths as our lips met, like he was trying to inhale the very essence of me. There are a lot of inferences I will take from people's body language, and this is one of them; I have always believed, like Cher, that having someone kiss you in and of itself means very little – it's *how* they kiss you that matters.

When I tried to remove his trousers, he said – this man who had told me all about the long days he spent campaigning for women's rights in his local housing development; who wore his feminist sweater in two of his five profile pictures; whose very identity was wrapped up in himself as feminist, as campaigner, as champion of equality – that he didn't want to go 'too far' because, 'I actually really like you.'

At the time I thought to myself, *How romantic – he wants it to really mean something when we sleep together*, but I'm a fool, because what he *actually* meant (and I know this because he literally told me this in words that came from his very own mouth) was, 'I don't want us to have sex and then for you just to be in the "sex" category.' It wasn't that he really, *really* liked me – it was that, in the world's least surprising news, he thought women who have sex on the first date are not 'girlfriend material'.

It wouldn't be too long a wait, anyway; we would have sex on our next date, the day he stood me up, after we spent an afternoon walking around a rainy Dublin, a day on which he refused to go for a coffee with me because 'that'll just give me anxiety', and insisted that we go to the cut-price supermarket and buy ingredients for dinner that we would then go home and cook. For once, I wasn't the only one bar-relling, at full speed, into a relationship.

It was odd, honestly – he made it clear that he wanted to be in a relationship with me, that he wanted to spend time with me, and that he would still want to spend time with me next week, and the week after, a security I don't remember ever feeling in a romantic relationship, in most of which it took at least six months for me to stop worrying about whether it was really 'going anywhere'.

At the same time he also made it clear that I had a lot of work to do on myself, which was made to seem somehow reasonable because, as he told me, so did he. He would put us both down frequently by mak-ing some sort of self-deprecating observation about *our* diets, or *our* bodies, or *our* career prospects. 'We're such fat bastards,' he'd say when our take-away delivery arrived – usually from the chipper or the Turkish grill around the corner. (He didn't like Indian food, or Thai, and it didn't matter to him that I did.)

Johnny

I remember feeling irked by the fact that, when-ever I would ask him, 'What do you feel like eating/doing/watching today?' he would simply answer the question, without asking what I wanted. I'm not sure why I never really made my own preferences clear to him; it was just a sort of mode we settled into. I accommodated him and he sort of ... put up with me.

Honestly, at the time, it seemed like a fair trade. When we first met, I was terrified that I had wasted five years of my life with Scott – that I would never meet anyone else who would love me as he had. If nothing else, a quick Google search would surely put them right off, revealing thread after thread of anonymous strangers detailing exactly why, and how much, they hated me.

After the first night that we slept together – and the sex was good, or as good as I had come to expect from my first time with a man, a first time that usu-ally happened a good three months before I felt comfortable enough to ask for a little more of this, a little less of that, 'not so much ... *jabbing*' – he got up and started to put his clothes on. It was dark out-side and in; his silhouette was illuminated by the yellow street light streaming through the blinds.

'I'll be going then!' he announced, chirpily, as if he was a plumber who'd just finished fixing my U-bend. He patted his jacket pockets, checking for something he couldn't risk leaving behind.

My face must have fallen because he turned to me then, almost aggressively inquisitive in his expression.

'What?! Is it not okay if I go?' he asked. I hesitated over my response. Honestly, I wasn't quite sure what was happening. I'd never slept with someone who had sought to exit the scene with such a sense of urgency. I was upset and taken aback but also confused – so confused at the actions of this man who had told me he wanted it to *mean something*, who had talked about the future with such casual assuredness, who had held my hand walking down Parnell Street.

He laughed, then, almost raucously. If life was a cartoon he would have been doubled over, red-faced. 'You should see your face!' he said and then, finally, located the carton of cigarettes he had left in his backpack. 'I'm just going to have a smoke. You coming?'

It felt as though he had revealed an absolutely undeniable truth about me: that I was pathetic and needy, and ridiculous, to boot, my insecurities never far from the surface.

That became a familiar pattern in our relationship. I would react – in hindsight, quite normally – to something he had said or done, and he would respond as if it was the funniest thing he'd ever seen, as if I was *the* most absurd human, for simply believing the words that came out of his mouth. He would pretend to get angry and then mock me for apologising for whatever slight had bothered him; he would feign indifference and then prod me in the ribs, saying, 'Oh, come on, have a sense of humour!' He was adept at convincing me that my feelings were always outrageously over the top, like he was a sort of jolly jester figure and I was the uptight ladies' maid who needed to be taught to enjoy life.

This is a common theme, I'm sure, but: it did not occur to me to consider this a problem of his making, an issue with his personality. After all, he had told me, all along, that *my* personality needed work. I genuinely thought that this was an adjustment period during which I would learn to stop taking myself so seriously. I thought he was going to be good for me.

There must have been moments in our relationship that were good and fun and affirming, that made me feel loved and wanted, because I remember telling my therapist at the time that I had never been with a man who spoke so freely about his feelings, who was so connected to his own emotions. After the emotional stonewalling that had been such a feature of the five years before we met, his ability to talk – exhaustively – about how he felt seemed refreshing. I felt optimistic about the life we would have together, with this open line of communication.

If there were warning signs at the time – and honestly, of course there were – it wasn't just that I was blind to them. I wilfully turned away. Clare tried to talk to me about his addiction, to warn me that there is no such thing as a 'cure', that it doesn't just go away, and I thought her old-fashioned; maybe addicts in *the olden days* were very likely to relapse, but Johnny was always talking about the coping tactics he had accrued. He was careful about who he was around; he didn't go to pubs, or clubs; he avoided the things he knew to be personal triggers. I believed him to be recovered, when I know now that he was actually in the process of recovering, a more complex, difficult and altogether delicate process that can – and should – last years, if not an entire lifetime.

He smoked a lot of weed, which he said quelled his anxiety. He would smoke a joint after breakfast, another before noon, a spare always in his wallet, just in case.

A few weeks into our relationship, I got a job as social media manager for a Dublin-based jewellery company, where I took photographs of diamond rings and lamented the chubbiness of my fingers, but in a friendly, warm office environment with a load of other women around the same age, people I would eventually come to think of as friends. He met me after work one day in what seemed to me to be a manic state, a level of high excitement I'd never before observed in him.

I should add a disclaimer to say: I am neither a psychiatrist nor a psychologist. But I knew what he was like and, on this particular evening, he was practically fizzing, frothing at the mouth, talking a mile a minute and almost vibrating with what felt a lot like poorly contained anger.

He told me that he had got talking to a guy on Instagram – there was a long, convoluted story about code words, letters and numbers by which each of them knew the other's intentions – who sold weed, and had gone to meet him on Dublin's Southside, in a car park by a well-known pub I used to pass on my way to a childhood friend's house.

In explanation, he told me that he owed too much money to his regular weed dealer so couldn't go to him, and was almost out. This guy was meant to have some incredibly high-grade weed. (There followed yet another long, convoluted story about THC and potency and other things I do not understand.)

The abbreviated version of it was that the man in question had sold him a large lump of dried oregano, wrapped in cling film, for the bargain price of €50. By the time Johnny realised what it was – I guess clandestine meetings for the purposes of buying drugs aren't exactly the place to thoroughly examine one's purchases – the trickster was gone. Johnny had, he told me, come back into town in a near-apoplectic rage, trying to devise a way to get revenge on this enterprising young herbalist.

'That's so annoying,' I said to him, feeling both empathetic – it truly is annoying to be tricked out of money – and also slightly amused. Oregano! Whoever would have suspected! Then, helpfully, I added, 'Oh, well.' Que sera, as they say!

Johnny wasn't really one for the que seras, as it happens; he began to tell me that no, it wasn't over – his friends were on the case.

'I told Kev and Ste to text him, tell him they want to buy some weed off him,' he said. 'Then they went and met him and boxed the head off him.'

'You . . . had him beaten up?' I asked incredulously.

'Yeah! He stole from me!' he said, bouncing lightly

on the balls of his feet, like a boxer getting ready for a fight.

'He stole ... fifty euro,' I said, slowly. He glared at me.

'Jesus fucking Christ, here we go – little miss priss, fifty euro's nothing, is it?! Maybe to you!' he said. He was still holding my hand, as if he wasn't shouting at me, walking down the street, as if he hadn't just told me that he had arranged to have some guy beaten up for swindling him out of €50 in a relatively low-stakes, dried-herb-related prank.

'Have you been drinking?' I asked him – which, for the record, is a question one must *never* ask an addict, although no one told me that because they were too busy telling me to stay away from him. People don't ever really help you navigate the thing they disapprove of, once they've finished telling you that you shouldn't be doing it in the first place. If you dismiss their advice, well, you're on your own, aren't you?

'What?! Fuck off!' he said. He didn't let go of my hand. 'Just because I'm annoyed means I've been drinking?! Fuck's sake!'

We went home then, ordered food, sat on the couch and watched Netflix. I don't remember speaking much, instead listening to him as he talked, quietly looking out for signs of ... I'm not sure what I was looking out for. He fell asleep right after he'd eaten, like a baby who'd become over-excited and collapsed in a fit of nervous exhaustion.

The following day, he told that he *had* in fact been

drinking; after he'd been robbed, he'd felt so angry and frustrated at having been taken advantage of that he'd gone into that well-known pub and ordered himself a Guinness. Just the one, he said, but one was enough, after months of abstinence, to make him feel its effects.

I didn't think to question the quantity itself, although now, looking back, I suspect that he'd had more than a single drink that night. It didn't seem to matter, either way; a drink was a drink, and a lie was a lie.

Needless to say, he didn't apologise for lying – and he maintained that he was right to sic his friends on the young guy with the oregano. How else would he learn?

That might have been the first sign – at least, the first I saw, the first I paid attention to – that things weren't going to work out between us. I started to write a short story about our doomed love affair. It started with the line, 'I should have known things weren't going to end well when he had a young guy beaten up for cheating him out of €50.' I'd never known anyone who would – or could – have someone else beaten up on their behalf or, if I did, they at least had the decency to keep it to themselves.

It may sound snobby, but I had always thought of there being 'types' of people who would do that, who would associate with people who resorted to violence so casually and so easily. I didn't know that I had any friends I could call to 'box the head off' someone who had done me wrong; I wasn't sure what it said about him, that he did.

That was the first time Johnny would admit to me that he had experienced a 'slip' in his addiction. It's what he called it, a 'slip'. He told me that he'd spoken about it at group, that they had all agreed it wasn't that big a deal, that it was understandable for him to have been angry, for him to have resorted to the one thing he had always relied on to dampen his emotions. He told me that they'd assured him this wouldn't in any way take away from how long he'd been sober. This moment of drinking alcohol, he said, didn't count. They'd told him so.

We had a handful of good weeks after that. It felt as though he was holding himself accountable, more than ever, keeping a close eye on his demons, walking as straight a line as he knew how – while still smoking weed and driving around with his delivery driver friend Kev at night, staying up till 3 a.m. and sleeping until lunchtime. His straight line was not the one I would have drawn for him, but he said it was working.

By Christmas time, we had been dating for a little over three months. We had not yet said, 'I love you'; I felt like it was coming, but I wasn't sure when. I did love him, I thought. He was funny and his hands were warm and he never pushed me to go out, or to dress up, when I didn't want to – partially, I can admit now, because when I did dress up he usually hated the outfit I'd chosen, or thought my makeup looked 'ridiculous'.

Johnny

His jealousy started to become an issue between us as Christmas loomed closer, and was exclusively directed at Liam, who was now, years after our failed attempt at a romantic relationship, one of my closest friends. As recounted earlier, we remained close, once the dust of our breakup had settled and we had stopped being angry with one another about who had done more laundry, or who always neglected to clean up after themselves. Our squabbles were almost always domestic.

Johnny had made it clear, very early on in our relationship, that he didn't want to know about anyone I had ever dated previously. I wasn't to bring them up; if I had a story that involved any ex-boyfriend, even my ex of five years, who was, naturally, a presence in a lot of my stories, I was not to share it with Johnny. 'It's not like I need to think you were a virgin before you met me,' he had once told me, unconvincingly.

For the first few weeks that we dated, he pretended that he was fine with my friendship with Liam, I think because he knew that he *had* to be fine. Liam was, at that stage, a permanent fixture in my life and, at least at the beginning, Johnny was not. We all had dinner together one night and they were polite and friendly to one another, laughed at each other's jokes. Afterwards, Liam said, 'He seems nice!' and I relayed this to Johnny, who asked, angrily, 'What's *that* supposed to mean? Did he think I wouldn't be?'

This was the beginning of the end for whatever burgeoning friendship I'd thought I could foist on them, the two most important men in my life.

By Christmas, then, Johnny had stopped pretending to have any time for Liam. Any stories that involved him were now *verboten* as well. I didn't talk about my podcast, which Liam produced; I didn't share with him any details of my week – coffees, lunches, long, laughter-soaked phone calls – that involved Liam. The world I shared with Johnny became smaller and smaller as my life became more and more compartmentalised. Not only was I careful about the things I shared with him, but I was careful about the things I *did*, too; if I knew it was something I couldn't tell Johnny about, it somehow felt like something I shouldn't have been doing in the first place.

Liam bought me a series of personalised Christmas gifts – a book he knew I'd loved as a child, an animated cel from one of my favourite childhood movies. Johnny's jealousy lingered in the air. I could taste it, acrid and rotten.

I didn't realise it at the time, but he was allowing his hatred and bitterness to fester. He had decided – perhaps because of how secretive he had forced me to become about Liam, about our conversations and the time we spent together – that I was having an affair. Liam was then living with his long-time partner, a man Johnny had also met, a man who had also laughed at Johnny's jokes.

It was all the more baffling to me because, if we had wanted to be together, surely we would be? It wasn't like I was staying with Johnny for the lavish gifts or holidays – he was living in his parents' house and working odd jobs for cash, almost all of which was spent on weed, or takeout food, or both – and Liam and I would have no reason to sneak around. Our friends and families – or at least mine, that I could be sure of – would have been delighted to see us reconciled.

In early January, I held my first book club meet-up for subscribers to my Patreon, a platform I had been working hard to build over the past few months, sharing personal essays and spending diaries that seemed to appeal to people's baser curiosities. Fifteen-odd participants had confirmed their attendance at an afternoon pizza-and-wine date, where we would discuss the book – Busy Philipps's *This Will Only Hurt a Little* – and whatever else came up.

I was excited, but also nervous. I had hosted one book club before, with a smaller number of people, in the more laid-back surroundings of the legendary Bewley's on Grafton Street. We had eaten cream cakes and drunk tea and coffee, and it had gone well, but without alcohol in the mix it had been a considerably tame affair. I wasn't quite sure how this one would go.

Johnny had come over earlier that afternoon to 'hang out', pretty much the only thing we ever did together. While I went to book club, he said, he wanted to go for a walk around town, take some photographs of the festive lights, the elaborate shop windows. Kev was going to be around; they might meet up for dinner. 'Have a great time!' he said, as I left the room. 'I'm really proud of you.'

It struck me, then, that this was an exceptionally

odd thing for him to say. Not, to be clear, for *any* boy-friend to say, but for this boyfriend, who was more likely to tell me, two minutes before it was time to leave, that I should change my outfit than that I looked great; who frequently said things like 'how you react to what I say is not my problem' when I suggested that he should perhaps be less critical, maybe a little kinder.

The book club went well. We agreed that we all liked Philipps a lot, although we weren't sure about the book, at least not entirely – 'very American', seemed to be the resounding review – but the pizza was good, and people laughed and it felt like a warm and positive and friendly place to be.

When I got home the house was in semi-darkness; Johnny wasn't home yet and Clare was in her room, reading a book and listening to music.

I called him to see where he was, what he wanted to do, and the voice that answered the phone sounded – to this untrained ear – distinctly slurred, drunk, out of it. He was shouting excitedly; told me he'd met Kev and they'd smoked a bong, that he was fine, on his way back now, 'See you soon!'

When he got to the house, he was, as I'd sus-pected, drunk, although, when pressed, 'What did you and Kev *do*?! Just some weed?', he insisted that they had met up, smoked a bong, had some food and gone their separate ways. It didn't occur to me, really, to wonder how and where they had smoked this bong – surely not in Kev's car – because it was such an obvious lie. It seemed surplus to requirements for me to attempt to poke holes in his story.

I'm not quite sure *how* Liam came up that night – like I said, I generally avoided mentioning him. I suggested, pretty soon after Johnny arrived, that he let me drive him home to sleep it off, and he immediately grew suspicious. Why? Where did I want to go? 'Oh, why don't you just go call your little friend *Liam*?!' (Liam, incidentally, is six foot one, not that it is in any way relevant but ... you know, men.) 'Yeah, go call your little *fag* friend Liam!' he repeated.

I felt myself harden. 'You need to leave,' I said, firmly. 'Oh, I'm leaving!' he said, beginning to pack up his bag, photography paraphernalia and cigarette papers tumbling out around him.

'No, I said, you really need to leave. This is done – this is over.'

He looked shocked.

'Oh *right*!' he shouted, voice dripping with venom. 'This is *over*. Great. Go and be with your fucking faggot friend Liam. You've always chosen him over me, that's fine – that is FINE.' More things got stuffed into the now-bulging backpack. Clare emerged, tentatively, from her bedroom, asked if everything was okay. I signalled for her to stay; I didn't want to be alone with him.

His exit was anything but graceful. He stomped down the stairs, attempting to get his backpack up on both arms, listing sideways into the wall and semi-sliding down the last few steps. As he opened the door, Clare grabbed me from behind. 'We can't let him go off alone like this,' she said. 'We should drop him home.'

We grabbed a key and followed him out on to the street, attempting to reason with him. 'Johnny!' I called, trying not to shout, not to make a scene – although really, the scene was set by then – as he strode purposefully off ahead of me, although not, worryingly, in the direction of his bus stop. 'Let me drop you home, please.'

'Come on, we'll give you a lift home,' Clare echoed, her voice a lot calmer than my trembling screeches. Johnny ignored us.

We finally caught up to him a few streets over, walking beside him as he tried to light a cigarette, mumbled to himself and then, at last, turned around to face us. 'I'm FINE!' he said. 'I'm going to go over to Liam's, we're gonna have this out, me and him! I'm gonna go over there and punch the head off him, I've had enough of this shit!' I tried not to laugh at the idea of it – Liam, in a fist fight! Johnny, managing to remember where Liam lives! – while being simultaneously horrified at what was unfolding.

'And you,' he said, leaning in close, 'can fuck! Off!' As he emphasised the last two words, he backhanded me on the chest. Two staccato slaps, not hard, but not light, either. I stepped backwards in surprise, my breast bone stinging slightly.

I tried again. 'Johnny! You don't even know where Liam lives, come on, let us drive you home,' I pleaded, although less certainly, this time – I did not, I thought, want to be in a car with this man. At this stage, I didn't particularly fancy being in an *arena* with him.

He laughed again, then turned and walked off,

shouting, 'I do know where he lives! First-floor apartment with the Pride flags in the window!' What had seemed ridiculous, almost laughable, mere moments ago, began to feel menacing, terrifying even, and utterly bizarre. It felt like a bad dream. Later, when I'd call a friend to tell her about it, I'd find myself laughing hysterically – at first she thought I was making it up. It simply didn't sound like something that could be true.

It's difficult to write about this night because it was so dramatic. It might have been the most dramatic night of my life, which depresses me to write down because it was not fun, or romantic, or exciting – all of the things that I would like to associate with the idea of The Most Dramatic Night of My Life. If I'd ever had to write an essay of that title during school, I could never have come up with anything this fantastical, or utterly heartbreaking.

Clare and I walked home, debating what to do. Doing nothing was one option; what were the chances that a very drunk and emotional Johnny would find Liam's exact apartment, figure out which buzzer was his, summon him downstairs and *actually* attack him? They seemed slim. But still ... he was right about the apartment being on the corner, on the first floor, about the Pride flag.

I called Liam to let him know about the nightmare unfolding in, now, both of our lives – he was out, having eaten dinner with his boyfriend, and they were walking home together, about five minutes from their apartment, bound to get there, I thought, before

Johnny did. I asked him if he wanted to come over to mine, but Johnny's threats seemed to spark a sort of protective pride in him, and he was determined to go home and stake out his territory.

Clare and I got in her car; I called Johnny, over and over, hoping that he would answer and I could figure out where he was, whether he was walking in the right direction, how long it would take him to get to Liam's and . . . I wasn't sure what he would do then.

He only answered once, to tell me, 'This is your fault, you know!' before hanging up immediately. I decided to try to get in touch with Kev; I didn't have his number but I followed his wife on Instagram, so I sent her a message. She got back to me almost immediately. When I called him, he told me that they had not, in fact, smoked any weed together; they'd had dinner, Johnny had seemed in okay form, then Kev had gone back to work and Johnny had gone, he'd said, to take some photos.

I filled him in on what had transpired and he asked for Liam's address; he would go there, he said, just in case Johnny turned up, and he could, hopefully, talk him down, bring him home.

We were minutes from the apartment when Liam called me. 'He's outside,' he said, slightly unnecessarily, as I could hear the shouts through my earpiece. He was on the street calling Liam's name, shouting, 'Come out and fight me!' like he was role-playing the part of a nobleman, challenging another for his lady's honour in a nineteenth-century romance novel, except without the romance part.

Liam's boyfriend Alessandro, he told me, wanted to go out and fight him. I suggested that this was, perhaps, not a great idea – although I did understand the sentiment. Liam said they were thinking of calling the police; I begged him not to, telling him that we were just around the corner.

When we finally pulled up, the shouting had stopped, and for a moment I thought maybe Johnny had given up and gone home, ambling back the way he'd come. Then I spotted him leaning against a wall opposite Liam's apartment block, the embers of his cigarette the only sign of life. I got out of the car.

His first reaction was surprise. 'How did you find me?!' he asked, as if he hadn't told me exactly where he was going, and why. I didn't answer.

'Johnny, you need to go home,' I said. 'Someone's going to call the guards.'

He made a kind of 'pfft' sound, waved a hand at Liam's window. 'Oh – he's gonna call the *guards* on me, is he?!' he said, incredulously, as if calling the police on someone who showed up outside your house threatening to beat you up was in some way a bizarre suggestion. I nodded.

Of course, I could have called the guards myself – and I probably should have. But I knew that wasn't something he would forgive, and I felt more sympathy for him than I did anger, at least in that moment.

He took a beat, then repeated his earlier conclusion. 'This is *your* fault!' he said, stepping towards me. I tried not to step back, remembering how he had, earlier, chosen to emphasise his point, my chest still stinging slightly, although mostly with shame. 'I loved you and you fucking couldn't just *not* with this . . .' he gestured at the window again. 'All you had to do was choose *me* over him and you couldn't fucking do that, could you?!' he asked. He was crying now, angry tears stubbornly making their way down his face. He didn't seem to notice.

I don't remember anything I said, if I said anything at all. I was crying too, at this stage – heartbroken at the thought of this rage he had been suppressing, unbeknownst to me, for so long; grief-stricken by the realisation that this was it, that there was no coming back from this moment for us, for our relationship; devastated that Liam, who had been such a good friend to me, was being dragged into this adolescent drama that was unfolding right outside his window.

Kev pulled up, then, and once again Johnny seemed shocked. 'What's *he* doing here?!' he asked, as Kev got out of his car. He pretty much took over negotiations, then, for which I was grateful – but sad, too, for him; I didn't get the impression that this was the first time he'd had to pick Johnny up and talk him down from a bad situation.

I made my way back to Clare's car, where we waited until Kev had ushered Johnny into his passenger seat and driven off. I called Liam again to let him know what had transpired and Clare and I drove home. We sat in the kitchen and had a drink, finished the leftover pizza I had brought home from book club (was that the same night?! It felt like years had unfolded between events) and I fell into a fitful sleep, waking now and then to come up with the various responses I would have for Johnny when he woke up from his bender and, inevitably, sent me dozens of grovelling text messages begging for me not to let this be the end of our love story.

There is a naivety that comes hand in hand with the very idea of being in love – a naivety that crosses over into hope, and is sometimes indiscernible from the other. The idea that this man who had, just the night before, told me he loved me, would *not* beg me to take him back, would *not* come to my door laden down with apologies and conciliatory gestures and words of assurance was almost as ridiculous as the memory of the night itself. It all felt like an impossibility.

Still, the following day passed without any communication from Johnny. Not wanting to make the first approach, I texted Kev to ask if he'd heard from him; he let me know that he'd spoken to him earlier that day. He seemed okay, Kev reported. He assured me that he wasn't worried about him, and I thought, neither for the first nor the last time, about how little time it seemed that Johnny spent worrying – or even thinking – about me.

It was the next day before I felt able to reach out to him, sending a short text. Simply: 'Are you okay?' Of course, I wasn't *really* asking if he was okay. I was reminding him that I was there, attempting to jolt him out of whatever black hole he had sunk into so that he would remember what had transpired. I needed him to acknowledge the trauma that had been inflicted on me, on my friends, for once to accept that *his* actions – rather than my reactions – had led to what felt like a kind of apocalyptic denouement of our relationship.

Satisfaction is never guaranteed, but never more so than when one imagines the response one might get to a text message. He didn't say anything about me, about Liam, about Clare or about Kev, the people who had been dragged around the city, following his irate rampage across town. Instead, he told me that he had gone to see his doctor that morning, that she had suggested he might have borderline personality disorder and undiagnosed bipolar disorder, prescribed him a series of heavy-duty pills, recommended that he speak to a psychiatrist.

He told me that, in the previous few weeks – unbeknownst to me – several of his regular jobs had fallen through; he had lost the social welfare payments he'd been receiving for the previous few months; he was worried about what he could possibly buy me for Christmas, how he could afford it, and felt that Liam's grand gift gesture had guaranteed that he could never compete.

The texts were coming thick and fast. He hadn't typed the word 'sorry' even once, but he was detailing the myriad reasons this latest 'slip' – he was still in recovery, he told me, and a one-night bender wouldn't change that – had been a long time coming.

'This can't be the end,' he finally beseeched me. 'Please tell me this isn't the end.'

A mere two nights previously, it had seemed very

much like the end. But now I began to second-guess myself.

As someone who suffers from mental illness, I have always worried about how my depression could impact – maybe ruin – my relationships. When I would go through particularly low periods, I would worry about when my ex would finally decide he'd had enough, that he deserved a relationship that was more carefree, less fraught with uncertainty and melancholy.

It hardly seemed fair that now, here I was, considering breaking up with someone whose own mental illness had caused them to explode so very dramatically – especially when, I assured myself, everything else had been going so well.

Plus – lest we forget – he had told me, however angrily, however influenced by the bottles of vodka he had managed to put away, that he loved me! That had to count for something. Love can build a bridge; love can conquer all; love lifts us up where we belong. I have never considered myself a romantic, necessarily, but I have always thought of love as something rare and special – and, regardless of how many niggling doubts were now eating away at my insides, surely this love that Johnny felt for me *meant* something.

With the benefit of hindsight, I am amazed by just how *shocked* my friends were when I told them that he wasn't well, that I had decided to support him, that he did not need to be pushed away, but rather to be comforted and assured that he had not burned his entire life to the ground in this one night of anger and threatened violence. Liam, I could tell, was angry – with Johnny, but also with me – although his was a quiet, disappointed rage.

'I don't want anything to do with him,' he said, and I accepted that – who could blame him? – while simultaneously feeling sad that these two men, both of whom I loved, would never be able to co-exist. What would happen at birthdays? Celebrations? If we got married, would Liam not come? (Could I expect him to?) I tried not to get ahead of myself.

'He's really ashamed of himself,' I told him. 'I think he needs some time, but I know he'll apologise to you.'

'I don't want him to, honestly,' Liam said, then. 'I honestly don't want to ever speak to him again – I don't even want to speak about him. I'm sorry—' I was embarrassed, then, as if he had anything to be sorry for '—but I can't hear anything about him, about your relationship. You'll have to find someone else to talk to.' Of course, of course.

Clare – who, granted, had not been threatened with bodily harm by my boyfriend – knew me well enough to understand my decision, but was also wary of our chances of success, whatever that might look like. 'Addicts don't just *change*,' she told me. 'He's selfish – and that's not his fault. If he wants to ever get better, he needs to just think about himself. And I want more than that for you.'

So did I, honestly, but with Johnny's new diagnosis, this treatment plan, the promise of a psychiatrist,

I felt that change was not only possible, but imminent. He's sick, I told myself, and he'll get better. And you can't just go and leave someone because they're sick.

Our relationship got back to a sort of familiar rhythm: takeaways on the couch, Johnny smoking weed to help him sleep, relax, work and generally cope with the anxieties that plagued him. He told me that he was on a new cocktail of antidepressants and tranquillisers and that, though his doctor had recommended he see a psychiatrist, the waiting list was long so he was continuing with his not-Alcoholics-Anonymous group therapy sessions, his sporadic one-on-one check-ins.

I didn't notice much of a difference in him except that he slept more. And though his financial troubles were never mentioned again, I started to pick up more and more of the tabs – granted, never for anything fancy, because now, more than ever, he did not want to go to restaurants, or to cafés, or even to the cinema. It was all too much for him, so we opted, again and again, for the quiet nights in.

I wasn't unhappy with all of this, per se. Nothing *bad* was happening, which had been my main concern after that night. He wasn't, to my knowledge, drinking again; he hadn't got into a rage in weeks; no wannabe drug dealers were being harmed. But I think, in all of this kind of downtime I was experiencing with him, I began to wonder about where I fitted in to this kind of life of rest and relaxation he was fashioning for himself.

In the silence that surrounded us so much of the

time, I didn't so much notice what was being said, but what wasn't. He never asked me how I was doing, or how my day was; he didn't talk about making plans for things we would do, or places we would go; there was never any concern, or even any recognition, of the fact that I might want something other than these Friday nights (and Saturday nights, and Sunday nights ...) on the couch, watching nature documentaries and waiting for the moment at which, inevitably, he would fall asleep with an open can of Coke at his elbow. I would carefully pluck it off the couch and place it on the coffee table, to prevent the calamity that was sure to come.

My own mental health wasn't really a feature of our relationship; we had talked about it in the early days, but as we had got closer and closer, it had been clear (to both of us, I'm sure) that his problems were greater than mine and, therefore, took precedence. If I was depressed, it didn't really matter because he was a lot more depressed than I was. I was, for once, the 'well' one in the relationship.

The peace was shattered – of course – by me, in the end. Lying in bed one Sunday morning, I decided to ask him if – as he had promised, in those difficult days after his BPD diagnosis, when he and I were both recovering from his bender – he had ever written to Liam to apologise. He had said he would write him an email. I had told him not to expect a response, and he had said that was fine, he understood. He knew that Liam was important to me, he had said.

My mistake became immediately apparent. Johnny,

having now spent weeks in a state of what looked a lot like calm reflection, was immediately defensive.

'Why?' he asked. 'Did he say anything?'

Liam had not said anything. I told him as much. 'He doesn't talk about you,' I said. 'We don't talk about you.'

'Well then, why are you bringing it up now?' he asked, and got out of bed, began to get dressed. 'What's the point in going over this? There's no point!'

'You said you'd apologise to him,' I insisted. I felt like a child. *But you said so!*

He sneered at me. 'Yeah – and what happens then?' he asked. He was almost shouting now (but not quite). 'I write to him, I say sorry, yadda yadda yadda, and he doesn't write back – and then I think about that for days, for weeks! I go over it *all* in my head and I'm right back to that day and I get set back *weeks* and for what? For him not to even fucking acknowledge me?!'

I was, once again, caught off guard by all of these thoughts he'd been having. I think, as someone who says almost exactly what she's thinking, almost exactly at the moment she thinks it, I have never quite managed to grasp the concept of people having such rich interior thought patterns. Mine are just so ... out there. That his were so very hidden from me felt like a shock.

'It's not about him *acknowledging* you,' I said, trying to stay calm, in the precise way that is guaranteed to enrage someone who is feeling distinctly not-calm.

'Well then, what is it about? You getting your way?'

I wasn't sure what to say to that. It wasn't about me getting my *way*, but it was about him keeping a promise. It was about him acknowledging that this had been difficult for me, that he had created a wedge between me and one of my closest friends, and that I had chosen to support him in spite of that.

Moreover, it was about Liam, whom he had actively tried to harm, and who deserved, at the very least, an apology.

'I spoke about it at group,' he said, and I felt a glimmer of hope. 'And they all agreed that I don't need to apologise for it. It's over. It's in the past.'

'But it's not in the past,' I said, once again confused by the whole ethos of this therapy group. 'You told me that you would do this thing, and—'

'Listen,' he interrupted me. 'I can't spend my life doing things for other people. I can't risk putting myself down a dark path again where who knows what will happen – I apologise and then I panic and then I hurt myself?' He shook his head, finished rolling his joint. He knew there was nothing I could say to that.

Once he'd smoked his joint and we were both deep into method acting that everything was okay, he suggested we go to the café on the corner for breakfast. This, we both knew, was his idea of a peace offering. *I know you're angry*, he was saying, *But how about a consolation prize?*

I knew, at that moment, that we were done. This was over. I had wanted to support him, but I couldn't face the idea of building a future with someone who couldn't – and wouldn't – ever countenance the idea of putting himself out in order to comfort, or support, the person he loved. (I did, for the record, believe that he loved me – but I simultaneously believed that he wasn't quite capable of the kind of love I had come to expect, the kind of love I felt I deserved.)

I am a coward, though, and so we went for brunch. I had the kale toast with a side of chorizo; he had the classic breakfast and complained about the smattering of watercress that was, he said, 'pretentious'.

Afterwards, I dropped him home. I told him I had work to do that day and couldn't come in; he didn't ask what work, or seem surprised that I suddenly had some work-related task to do on a Sunday. Maybe that was just another thing he couldn't find space for. He gave me a kiss goodbye and walked inside without looking back.

The breakup itself happened, then, kind of accidentally. I had decided that I would drop over to his house after work one day that week. I wanted him to be in his home environment, with people he loved, when we had the conversation I was dreading. I didn't want him to be in the city, surrounded by the temptation of pubs and clubs and off-licences, while he was caught off-guard with news of my abandoning him.

But he must have known, because when I suggested dropping over to him, he asked why; why wouldn't he just come to mine, as usual; what did I want to say; why didn't I just say it now; could I talk; could he call me? (He never called me. 'Phone calls give me anxiety,' after all, and so we didn't speak on the phone for our entire relationship.) I was at work, so I took the call in a conference room just off the corridor that led to our shared office space.

'What's going on?' he asked, in an eerily cheerful, reasonable tone. Then: 'You're not breaking up with me.'

'I don't want to do this any more,' I said, quietly (like I said, a coward).

'Why?' he asked. Again, he sounded very calm – I was suddenly glad that we were not having this conversation in the isolation of his childhood bedroom.

'I just . . . Do you know, you never ask how I am? Or how my day went? You never ask about me,' I told him. Immediately, I felt this was a mistake. What if he argued? What if he promised to change? What if he told me he'd do better, *be* better? Would I be strong enough to insist on walking away?

I needn't have worried.

'I don't ask *anyone* how they are!' he said. 'Not my friends, not my family . . . I just can't. I can't take that on! Like, what if you tell me you're feeling shit, and you're having a shit day? I have my own shit to deal with. I need to focus on that. I can't let someone else's shit drag me down. I know how *that* ends.'

I heard Clare, once again, telling me about how addicts needed to be selfish.

'I'm sorry,' I told him. 'But that's not good enough for me.' I once again braced myself for his entreaties, his apologies, promises he would make that I would probably believe.

'Okay,' he said. 'If that's what you want.'

'That's what I want,' I confirmed.

He said okay again, and then goodbye. We hung up.

Of course, nothing's really over until it's over – and Johnny had left a lot of his things at my house. I guess it's inevitable, when you spend weekends at a time on someone's couch, that they will accumulate some of your belongings. Socks and underwear would, I'm sure, have been happily left behind – but I also had jumpers and T-shirts, one of his camera lenses, a handful of books, a pair of sunglasses.

I texted him, a week or so after our breakup, and offered to drop them over to his house.

'You're grand!' he said (the exclamation mark should have been a warning sign). 'I'll drop in and get them on Friday, I'm meeting Kev in town around 7.'

On Friday, he arrived at 6.45 p.m. I was waiting, pacing nervously around the house, straightening picture frames and fluffing cushions and wondering how this would go. Would I cry? Would he? Clare was upstairs, getting ready to meet a friend in a nearby pub for drinks and a trivia night. I had been invited, but I felt as if I was in a form of recovery of my own. I was reclaiming my couch, my Friday-night takeaways. I was looking forward to this night alone, just me, my dog and my thoughts.

It was apparent, the minute he came through the door, that he was not just drunk, but very, *very* drunk. He pulled me immediately into a hug, smiling broadly, asked how I was. I'm not sure that I even responded.

'You look great!' he said effusively. (I didn't, and I was immediately enraged about all of the times he'd told me, straight out, that I looked terrible – *now* was the time he chose to lie?)

I picked up his bag of stuff, stuttered something about his things, his lenses, his jumpers.

'Oh, you could have kept that!' he said, spotting a bright blue jumper I had taken to wearing around the house while we were still together.

'No, no, that's yours,' I said nervously.

He pulled me into another hug. 'I'll always love you, you know,' he said. 'Like – *you*. Not Rosemary Mac Cabe you, but *you*-you.' I didn't tell him that we were one and the same; I think I just said thank you.

'Look after yourself,' he said, then, and let himself out the front door. Clare emerged from her room, then, as I crumpled on to the bottom step and began to cry.

'It's so sad,' she said, hugging me tightly. 'It's really sad.'

I hadn't got my phone on me, then, or for the next twenty or so minutes while we discussed Johnny's fleeting visit in the bathroom, as Clare applied her eyeliner and perfected her red lip. I picked it up just as she was about to leave and noticed that I had four missed calls from Johnny, a voicemail, three texts. I listened to the voicemail on loudspeaker, not sure what to expect.

His voice was garbled, by the wind or the drink I couldn't quite tell. 'Is this ... supposed ... a *joke*?

Vodka?!' he said. '... not funny!' The voicemail ended. I opened the texts.

'Is this supposed to be a joke?' read the first.

'Why would you put a bottle of vodka in my bag?!' The second.

The third was a photograph of a shoulder of Huzzar vodka, propped on top of his blue jumper, beside his boxer shorts.

A fourth text came through. 'Are you going to answer me?!' My phone began to ring.

'Jesus,' said Clare. 'Are you okay?!' (I was not okay.)

Lest it need to be said: I had not put a bottle of vodka in among Johnny's things. As I told my sister over the phone later that night, I have never bought Huzzar vodka – I'm not quite at Grey Goose levels, but I'd be forking out for Smirnoff, at least, or Absolut.

I received a further dozen or so texts that night, and a handful of phone calls. I decided to go with Clare to the pub, not wanting to risk the possibility of Johnny coming back to the house to confront me. We performed admirably badly at trivia, which was space-themed. Alas, it was less 'space: the final frontier' and more 'space: NASA and stuff', which placed me at a serious disadvantage.

I was almost tempted to get up on stage, steal the microphone from the announcer and tell everyone that I was not, in fact, inept but had actually just had a *very traumatic few weeks*, thank you very much. (It occurred to me, much later on, that my teammates did not have any such excuse and should genuinely have been ashamed of themselves for their embarrassingly low score.)

A few weeks later, Johnny's birthday came around. I hadn't heard from him since the Huzzar vodka incident. I don't know why, but I had expected to – thinking he might sober up and realise what an idiot he'd been, I'd been expecting an apology text to come through at any minute. Instead, silence.

I decided to text him 'happy birthday', not because I wanted him to have a happy birthday – I was done being nice, in all honesty – but because I wanted him to feel ashamed. I wanted to force him to acknowledge how badly he'd behaved, to sheepishly apologise for coming to my house drunk, for accusing me of . . . what exactly? Trying to jeopardise him?

He wrote back almost immediately. 'Thanks R!'

I deleted his number.

Brandin

I'm not sure if I'll ever feel comfortable calling Brandin my husband – despite the fact that we are, in fact, married. I just call him Brandin or, if I'm writing more generally about my life, I'll refer to him as my American because he is that, too: American and, I guess, mine.

We met on Tinder in the early summer of 2019, while I was on a three-week holiday to visit my sister in the American Midwest, where she lives with her husband and their four boys. I was still all at sea after my breakup with Johnny, and feeling a little aimless in terms of life and work – this book had been commissioned, then in the form of a series of letters to my exes, but otherwise I wasn't quite sure what I was at, or where I was going.

Despite the fact that I am, historically, excellent at finding and securing myself a boyfriend when the need strikes, I had started to think that maybe I would spend my life in a series of long-term serious relationships. I'd thought, after all, that Scott and I were going to get married, and now that the fog was beginning to clear after both that and my breakup with Johnny, I was trying to work on resigning myself to the fact that my life might end up looking different to how I'd hoped.

I was also thirty-four, or 'in my mid-thirties' – it was a good six years since I'd been told about my low egg count, and I couldn't imagine my reproductive prospects had improved in that time – and I was quickly approaching the age at which the words 'geriatric pregnancy' would be bandied around, even if I did, miraculously, manage to get pregnant. Not to mention the fact that, for that to happen, I'd have to have either a man or a whole bucket full of money, and neither of those things seemed particularly likely to fall out of the sky any time soon.

It was during that trip that my sister suggested that I apply for a visa to come to the US. I'd been telling her about this new type of visa that was available to freelance content creators; I had seen several of my peers apply for, and be granted, that very same visa, in order to post their outfit-of-the-day photographs against a glamorous New York City backdrop.

This wasn't the first time she had suggested that I move abroad, at least for a few months. She had moved to Italy the month she graduated from college, while I had always been a real homebody; she seemed to think that a few months out of Ireland would be good for me, in the way that people suggest things you really don't want to do under the guise of self-improvement.

She lived in Brooklyn for a few years when her

eldest son was born, and had urged me to come and spend some time with her there, but New York scared me. It was too busy and too hectic and there was always someone shouting at someone else in a way that felt truly mortifying. (I suspect that's the Irish in me.)

When she lived in Dallas, she brought me in for a meeting at the company she was working for, with a view to working with them on their social media strategy. I never followed it up and she didn't push it; I think she knew that I, with my long-term boyfriend and my lovely little house in town, was unlikely to up sticks and leave it all behind for a corporate job in Texas.

But now, things were different. I was, for the first time in as long as either of us could remember, single. I had been renting in the same house in Dublin for seven years – I once did the maths and worked out how much I'd paid in rent to my landlord, which was galling – and my career was, also for the first time, entirely remote.

I was writing a paid newsletter for subscribers only and recording a weekly interview podcast, while occasionally contributing freelance articles to a handful of Irish newspapers and magazines.

There was, as they say, nothing keeping me in Ireland.

In a very on-brand move, one of the first things I did was join Tinder. Even before I had engaged the services of a lawyer to discuss getting a visa that would allow me to work in the US – I had arrived on a tourist visa, and could not work while I was visiting my sister – I thought, *If I'm going to think about living in Indiana, I may as well get an idea of the local talent.* Maybe I'd find my happily ever after in the bustling metropolis of Fort Wayne. Stranger things have happened, surely.

I first went on a date with a married man named Austin, who was, he told me, in an open relationship. He had three young children and his wife was 'very cool' with the idea of his dating other people. He even invited me to come shooting on his land (what is it with me and conservative chino-wearers?), which gave me some reassurance that he wasn't carrying on behind her back.

In one of his photos, he wore a novelty three-piece Christmas suit; in another, he was holding the hand of a small, smiling toddler. Once we had exchanged numbers, he called me on the phone. 'It's easier to have a decent conversation, don't you think?' I most certainly did not think; I had only answered out of sheer fright and panic. No one ever called my phone except my doctor's surgery.

We went on one date, for dinner to a downtown microbrewery where I drank raspberry beer – back to my old ways – and asked him questions about life in Fort Wayne. He revealed to me, midway through our meal, that he did, in fact, have *four* children, the youngest of whom was ten weeks old. 'I thought it might sound bad . . .' he mumbled. It *did* sound bad.

It turned out that he and his wife had been married for five years and had four children. 'As soon as we got married, she lost interest in sex,' he confided. The fact that she had been pregnant, or immediately postpartum, for the entire duration of their marriage seemed an irrelevance to him.

'Do you not feel bad,' I asked him, 'that your wife's at home with three kids and a tiny baby while you're out on a date?'

He bristled slightly.

'She gets time off, too!' he protested. I couldn't help but wonder whether her time off involved being wined and dined in the local bar, or if he simply watched his own children while she took a bath or washed her hair. I strongly suspected the latter.

In any case, I am a coward so I didn't push the issue, and when he dropped me home and walked me to the back door of my sister's house, I was fully prepared for the goodnight kiss that I could feel was coming.

As we approached the back door – I didn't have my own key to their house yet, so she had stayed up to let me in – we were illuminated by the lamp in their sitting room, where my sister sat in her dressing gown. She was like a deer caught in the headlamps; we were the large, American SUV, disturbing her peace.

All of a sudden I was mortified by the sight of us both: me, in a nice dress and a pair of sandals, having painted my toenails for the occasion; him, in a pair of pressed, bootcut jeans with a dusty pair of brown leather sandals. She was never going to let me live this down.

Of course, I underestimated her; though she got great mileage out of the jeans-and-sandals combo, it was the open marriage and the ten-week-old baby that truly drew her ire. 'I mean ... you're not thinking of seeing him again, are you?!'

'No, no!' I said, weakly, knowing well that any whiff of enthusiasm from Austin would reduce any resolve I had to dust in a millisecond.

Sure enough, he texted me that night to tell me what a great time he had. 'I think you're really great!' he said, and I started to imagine my life as girlfriend to this happily married man.

Over the next few days, I texted him on the sly, keeping my phone face down at all times, lest his name pop up and my cover be blown. But there's a reason I don't play poker: I am an utterly terrible liar, and when my sister asked, 'Who are you texting?' there was no fooling her.

It was, honestly, the shame of it that caused me to cut things off with him, after that one snog-free date – my sister was feeling incredibly sympathetic towards his 'poor wife', and hating him a lot, but she was also incredibly pragmatic about his prospects.

'What would you get out of this, exactly, aside from the odd night out?' she asked. 'You'll just fall in love with him and he'll still be married, with his four kids and his wife, and you'll just be his bit on the side.'

Anyone who has an older sister will know how painful this is to commit to paper: of course, she was right.

Brandin was the second, and last, local man I'd go

out to eat with. His Tinder profile showed him as divorced, with two young children – boys (why couldn't I have met a nice man with a daughter?! I long for a girl to practise my braiding skills on) aged three and five – and a penchant for ridiculous outfits. In one of his photographs he wore a kilt with an old, faded band T-shirt. When I asked if this was fancy dress, he responded, simply, 'No, my family's Scottish.' *Americans!* I thought, with an eye-roll.

We met for lunch at Buffalo Wings & Ribs, a local chain restaurant which specialises in, you guessed it, chicken wings, the universally accepted *worst possible* first-date food. I must admit, it was my fault; on my dating profile, along with a brief *Star Wars* mention, I had also said that I loved chicken wings, something that is not so much a lie as a fact about me carefully chosen to appear attractive to members of the opposite sex. *Plus ça change, plus c'est la même chose.*

My sister dropped me at the restaurant – he had offered to drop me home – and she and my then two-year-old nephew, Fox, waved me off as I approached him. He had waited outside the restaurant for me, leaning against one of the stone columns that seems to adorn every strip mall in this city.

He was wearing a very bright aqua-blue polo shirt and a pair of khaki shorts, with sneakers, a choice for which I was grateful after the ribbing I'd got over Austin's sandals. Later, Brandin would admit that he simply couldn't find sandals big enough to fit his cursedly giant feet, but in that moment it seemed more like a blessing.

Months later, Brandin would tell me that he knew, that day, over chicken wings and Diet Mountain Dews, that he had fallen in love with me. All I knew was that he was incredibly affable and easy to talk to, asking as many questions as he answered.

He told me about his kids and his divorce; how he'd taken up crochet to fill the time, now that he lived alone; about the weightlifting gym he'd recently joined. I told him about the differences between Ireland and the US; how I'd never drunk a Mountain Dew; and about Austin, the married dad of four looking for a girlfriend.

'What a jerk,' he said, not inaccurately.

After lunch, we grabbed drive-thru coffees and sat in his car, talking, as the afternoon turned to dusk. It was one of those early summer days in the Midwest that's roasting in the afternoon, but cools rapidly as the sun sets. I drank my coffee black, back then, still too intimidated by the Starbucks menu to ask for anything I thought of as 'fancy'; he ordered a peppermint mocha and I thought, *Ugh*. I've never been one to pay attention to red flags, and a peppermint mocha is, I can admit, a minor infraction.

I spent the duration of our coffee-drinking time in his car, I hope giving the impression of someone listening carefully to his conversation while also trying to read whatever signals he was subconsciously giving off. His hand brushed my hand – was that by accident? Eye contact is very good. Does that even mean anything? Surely he wouldn't be hanging out with me for the entire afternoon if he wasn't a little interested . . .

Still, he drove me home to my sister's house and we didn't so much as hug goodbye. I hopped out of his enormous truck – Americans and their cars, honestly – as gracefully as I could with a smile and a thank you and went inside to regale my sister with all the not-at-all-sordid details.

I heard from him later that evening – a text to say that he'd had a wonderful time, and to ask if I'd like to do it again.

For our second date, we went to what has now become my favourite restaurant in Fort Wayne, a kind of hard-to-describe fusion restaurant that combines elements of Asian cooking with accents of barbecue (I told you, hard to describe) and does *the* best burgers. Afterwards, he took me on a walking tour of downtown and showed me the 'historic' buildings – I am slowly learning not to scoff when Americans use the word 'historic', often meaning something that is more than ten years old and not built entirely from prefabricated pieces – from what used to be a classic hotel and is now a bank to the courthouse where, two years later, we would say our 'I dos' from beneath mask-covered faces.

Something that is perhaps relevant to this particular part of the story: Brandin is six foot six. I am five foot six. Having been forewarned of the planned walking tour, I had worn flat shoes on our date, so any potential lip-locking was severely thwarted by the height difference.

As we walked around, I kept wondering if it would be weird for me to hop up on a step, in the doorway of some closed shop – all the better to kiss him, obviously – but it all seemed too forced. At some stage throughout the evening he had reached for my hand. It felt both innocent and lovely, a bit like what I imagine dating would have been like in the 1950s, except that I was wearing a giant, patterned shirt dress and neither of us was smoking.

By the time we pulled up in my sister's driveway in the late evening, I was determined not to let him go home without so much as a short snog, so I asked if he'd like a coffee. It was a beautiful evening – warm and clear – and we sat by the pool drinking our Nespressos, watching the fireflies bob up and down across the grass.

'We don't have them in Ireland!' I told him, a sentence that would soon become my most-used refrain. On the list: fireflies, guns, instant chocolate pudding, white eggs that need to be refrigerated, snow ploughs, opossums, stink bugs and a thousand other things I was not prepared for.

The perfect moment – the one where our eyes would meet and we'd lean in towards one another for the perfect kiss – did not arrive. One or other of us was talking at all times, and as the darkness set in, threatening to obscure one another's faces entirely, I decided to just go for it mid-sentence, and went in for the kill.

We 'made out', as we say in America, for what felt like hours – and I couldn't help but feel slightly aggrieved that he made absolutely no effort to feel me up. I was wearing a sort of mini muumuu, a dress which, though it was slightly longer in the back, stopped a good few inches above my knee in front, for crying out loud. It was the perfect dress for a bit of a late-night grope by the pool, but no!

I didn't realise it at the time, but Midwesterners are far more polite than us Irish people, perhaps because we've learned the art of courtship through a cloak of inebriation. Most of the romantic moves we make have been learned while emboldened by alcohol, after all (some stereotypes are true), and we are not used to the kind of well-mannered slow-and-steady romance I was now being offered.

As it happened, Brandin and I would keep our relationship in the innocent make-out stage for several months. I was nervous about the inevitable long distance that would soon be between us, and afraid that absence would, in fact, make the heart grow less fond, and that I would somehow blame the fact that I had slept with him, should he decide he wasn't keen on me after all.

I don't know if I will ever get over the suspicion that men categorise women by their levels of sexual availability, and that the more available you are, the more firmly you are placed in the 'casual' box.

In a way, this approach also helped to somehow mark our relationship out as being about something more than physicality, which was, after all, the measure by which I had always determined a man's interest in me. Without sex to muddy the waters, we got to know one another more thoroughly and honestly than we would have otherwise, I think.

In all, I spent six months of that year (the maximum time allowed under my tourist visa) in the US. I joined the same weightlifting gym Brandin had been going to and went there three mornings a week, borrowing my sister's car on the proviso that I act as her chauffeur, ferrying her to and from her office, a ten-minute drive from the house.

After my workout, I would go to one of two restaurants downtown – one, a restaurant that served the most delicious breakfast tacos, the other, a café that did excellent coffee and a crème brûlée French toast that will forever rank in my top three favourite French toasts. (The other two are to be found in Dublin establishments: one comes with mascarpone and buttered bananas, while the other is stuffed with rhubarb and berries.) There, I would scoff breakfast delicacies, work on this very book or my newsletter, and liaise with my lawyer, whose list of must-haves for my visa application grew longer with each passing week.

When I went home, after that first visit, with a return trip planned for October, and another at Christmas, Brandin brought me to the airport. He walked me to the security queue and we kissed and he told me that he would miss me but not, as I had been expecting – and hoping – that he loved me. I was sure he did; he had made several allusions to it, without going so far as to make it explicitly clear. But I needed to hear the words.

I cried as I walked to my gate, disappointed and

worried about this time apart, a worry that was compounded by the fact that I didn't know whether or not my visa would be granted at all.

The process itself was neither straightforward nor cheap; nor was it speedy. In all, I think it was eight months before I was ready to submit my application, and a further two months until it was approved and I was on a flight to begin my three-year stint in the United States of America.

In order to apply for, and have any hope of being granted, the visa I was applying for, the 'extraordinary alien' visa, I had to show that I was, in fact, an extraordinary alien. So alongside my own documentation – my birth certificate, passport, proof of income and so on – I was tasked with finding eight to ten 'noteworthy' individuals who would write letters of recommendation for me, telling the relevant authorities how 'essential' my voice was, and how much I would contribute to the US cultural landscape by basing my work there.

My lawyers drafted template letters in the style required by these types of visa applications. I then sent them to the people I'd asked – an author I admired and with whom I was connected via social media; a magazine editor I once worked for; a radio show host who happened to be a friend of the family.

As I sent them, I made sure to point out that I was aware of how gushing they sounded. 'Feel free to edit as you see fit!' I wrote. 'My US lawyers wrote these for me.'

One recipient responded almost immediately. 'Rosemary,' they wrote, 'I'm sorry but I could never sign something like this! I absolutely could not put my name to it – I'll have to rewrite it!'

I didn't write back straight away, allowing the red mist of rage and humiliation to dissipate before reiterating, 'Of course! I did say it was pretty gushing – make whatever edits you need!'

In the end, their edits were minor; I think it may have simply been important to them to clarify, both to themselves and to me, that they didn't think I was all that great.

I have never found long-distance romance to be a satisfying state of affairs, and I honestly don't believe that absence makes the heart grow fonder. For me, absence makes me forget exactly what it is that drew me to the person in question – and the longer it goes on for, the easier I find it to imagine a life without them.

It also causes me to grow increasingly paranoid and insecure. I required constant reassurance from Brandin that he was missing me; that he thought this time spent apart would be worth it, when (and if) we could eventually be together; that he was serious about our relationship.

What I began to learn about Brandin, during this time spent apart, talking on the phone each evening as I lay in bed and he drove home from work, is that he is incredibly straightforward. That being said, he is not massively intuitive. He did not pick up on my subtle signals as I attempted to elicit from him the assurance that he was still invested in our relationship, but when I eventually told him exactly what was going on in my head, he was quick to respond.

'I'll wait for however long it takes,' he told me. 'I have absolutely no interest in anyone else.'

I returned that October for six weeks, and again at Christmas with my parents, to spend the festive period with my sister and her family. Brandin and I spent more and more time together. He introduced me to his sons and we went to the playground together; drove downtown for burgers; spent evenings watching movies in his living room.

We slept together, too, when I made that second trip to Fort Wayne. We had been dating, long distance, for about five months, and the longer it went, the more I worried that, when we did finally have sex, it would be a disappointment for us both.

As it happens, I need not have worried. If there is one thing guaranteed to make any sexual experience a success in my mind, it is feeling like I am *wanted*, like I have fulfilled the desires of my sexual partner. The fact that we had been building up to this moment for months meant that our enthusiasm levels were off the charts. We fell into one another, breathed sighs of relief as we finally came together.

We didn't, of course, *come* together. This is not a romance novel. He came first, and then I said, with a confidence I didn't quite feel, 'My turn.' He brought me to orgasm with his hands, and some constructive encouragement. I had a strong feeling that this was going to be something serious, and I was determined not to make the same mistakes I had in the past.

I had never previously considered the idea of dating someone who already had children – I thought I would always be slightly envious of the attention they paid their kids, which feels like an embarrassing thing to admit – but everything was different in this new American life. *I* was different.

Not being sure whether I would ever have children of my own, it seemed almost fated that I would meet this man, these boys, this ready-made family, and slot right in.

I finally sent through my completed visa application in January 2020, the week after my parents and I flew back home to Ireland, having spent Thanksgiving and Christmas with my sister and her family. By February, it had been approved and I booked my flight to the US for 20 March 2020, with a return flight in May to come home for a friend's wedding.

In a way, I was surprised at myself and how happily I had come to the decision to move, but I was also determined to fly home at least twice, if not three times, each year. I could, after all, work from anywhere, and I had a life in Ireland that I was not planning to fully abandon.

What is it they say about the universe laughing at the plans we make? By 13 March, news broke of then-president Trump's Covid-related ban on travel from Europe, which would come into effect in the next few days. I bumped my flight forward a week and packed my cases in a panic, landing in Chicago to a line for immigration that was several hundred people deep, complete with temperature checks and detailed screenings.

Brandin had come to pick me up, and by the time I made it through to the arrivals hall, he had been waiting for seven hours. He had spilled coffee on his shirt, and parked in a car park that was a shuttle bus away – a bus for which there was yet another long queue.

'Why didn't you move the car while you were waiting?' I asked, somewhat ungratefully – he had, after all, driven three and a half hours to wait a further seven for his Irish girlfriend to make it off her plane. He shrugged.

'I didn't know how long you'd be!'

I fell asleep on the drive home, despite promising I'd keep him company. Ordinarily, I'd fall asleep on a plane within seconds of takeoff, but nothing about this trip had been ordinary and I had been too on-edge to doze off until now.

We got back to his house at 4 a.m. and collapsed into bed, not to emerge until noon the following day.

I wouldn't get home to Ireland for more than two years.

For the first six months of my time in the US, I lived in my sister's spare bedroom, regularly being awoken by the tiny hands of my nephew, Chance, who was four at the time.

'Open yo eyes!' he would tell me. 'It's maw-neen!'

Brandin and I, after our initial few days reconciling, had decided to socially distance from one another during those early pandemic weeks. While the rest of the world was working remotely from home, Brandin was still required to go into his office, where masks were not mandatory, and we all felt that it would be safer for us to stay away, rather than increase the risk of letting Covid into our little seven-person bubble (one of whom, Fox, was just two, and had experienced, in his early years, a respiratory condition that we worried would put him at much higher risk of serious illness, should he catch the virus).

Luckily, I had arrived as the weather began to turn, from the freezing-cold snowy winter that seems to last six months in the Midwest, to the hot summer that allows for regular barbecued dinners and days spent by the pool.

Brandin would come over in the evenings and we would sit outside on the patio, drinking coffees or Diet Cokes and chatting about whatever we had forgotten to tell each other via text during the day. In the summer months, he brought his boys over at weekends and we would each pick a side of my sister's pool, spending the ensuing hours shouting, 'Six feet apart, please!' at children who really could not have cared less.

I found those first months difficult, as the reality began to set in that I might not get home for months, even a year or so, and I felt as if I was being forced to make a firm decision – here or there – when I had hoped that I would get to test the waters, so to speak, while I ran down the clock on my three-year visa.

I would speak my fears aloud to Brandin – what if my parents got sick? What if I never got to eat a decent flaky pastry ever again? – and he would respond in his characteristically calm and pragmatic manner.

'Babe,' he said to me once – yes, we are the couple that call one another babe, something that initially embarrassed me, but now I think, fuck it – 'if you need to go home, I understand.'

'But I won't be *able* to come *back*!' I snivelled; the travel ban, such as it was, would not have allowed me to re-enter once I'd left, as I was neither a permanent resident nor a Green Card holder.

'I know,' he said. 'It's okay.'

It turns out that a leopard cannot change its spots, because what I heard, in those words, was: 'It's okay if you never come back because I don't really love you.'

Though Brandin had never really given me a reason to doubt his feelings for me, I still required near-constant reassurance that he *wanted* and *needed* me. I had previously found the intense love of my teenage years too much, but this calm, decided love of my thirties was feeling like it might just be too little.

When I expressed this to him – one thing my thirties have at least eliminated is any desire to seem 'cool' and 'nonchalant' – he laughed, like a man with a death wish.

'What?!' he spluttered, somewhat incredulously. 'Of course I want you to stay! I love you! But I would hate to feel like you stayed for me when you really wanted to go home.'

We had many such misunderstandings, if you could call them that. Rather, they were moments where I set out a forked path in front of him, in the guise of some dilemma or other. Turn left and you are telling me that you love me; turn right and I'll know you don't really give a shit.

He chose right, over and over again.

And yet. I think, in my relationship with Brandin, I have learned that you cannot force someone to show you how they feel, at least not in the specific way you think they should. He is a very straightforward person; he tells me that he loves me every night before bed, and sometimes at random moments, when I'm petting the dog or playing *Candy Crush* on my phone or attempting to remove one of the thick, dark hairs that has, in the last few years, taken up residence on my chin.

But he doesn't do a lot of the things I had once expected would come with *being* loved. He doesn't buy me gifts, unexpectedly and for no reason. He doesn't write long, effusive love notes on my birthday or Valentine's cards (but he does, at the very least, give me cards with short inscriptions contained therein). He doesn't tuck my hair behind my ear and tell me how beautiful I am; or massage my shoulders as he walks by, ending with a kiss on my neck; or sigh as we kiss and tell me how lucky he is. Hollywood has, obviously, a lot to answer for.

We moved in together in the summer of 2020 and I went from social distancing from him to social distancing from my sister and her family, which was more of a challenge. While Brandin and I were apart we texted pretty regularly; we spoke on the phone every night; we saw one another, albeit at a distance, several times a week.

As it happens, my nephews are rubbish at phone conversations, and texting them is futile (they don't have phones). My sister and I spoke regularly, of course, but it wasn't the same, and I was glad when, that Thanksgiving, we decided to relax our boundaries and see one another, aware of the risk that entailed.

We spent the holidays – as they say here, in this new land – together, FaceTiming my parents over our turkey and potatoes. This was the longest they had ever gone without seeing any of their grandchildren, and they had spent most of the year in near complete isolation, acutely aware that they, being in their seventies, were in the highest category of risk.

We marked New Year's Eve by doing ... nothing at all. Brandin had gone out earlier that day to drop off something he'd borrowed from a friend and I had stayed home, drinking lukewarm tea at the kitchen table while I attempted to complete a 1,000-piece puzzle: a floral arrangement I'd been given by a friend and which was, I was convinced, missing a crucial piece.

When he got home, I barely looked up from my puzzle; I asked, half-heartedly, how his drive was and then if he would help with my jigsaw, a constant request that had, without exception, always elicited the same negative answer.

'Sure,' he said, and then, crouching down beneath the kitchen table, 'I think there's a piece under here.'

Well, you can only imagine my delight: my missing piece! Under the table! I turned to look at him, by now on one knee, holding not a puzzle piece but a small, square box. I was confused. I glanced at him, then at the floor. *But . . . my puzzle piece.* I glanced at him again.

I had never really imagined what it would be like to be proposed to, properly, with a ring and everything – but I certainly hadn't thought it would come like this, in our kitchen, with its neon yellow walls (he had 'redecorated' the house himself when he moved in, a few months after his divorce), while I did a jigsaw puzzle, wearing an oversized woolly jumper and a pair of lemon yellow sweatpants I had bought on the advice of a frankly misleading plus-sized influencer (gorgeous on her; heinous on me).

'Are you serious?! Is this a joke?!' I asked, feeling at once delighted and also deeply embarrassed, convinced there was a hidden camera somewhere in the room.

'It's not a joke,' he said, and laughed. 'Well?'

'You haven't *asked* me anything!' I scream-laughed at him.

'Rosemary no-middle-name Mac Cabe,' he said (he fixates on the weirdest things, honestly). 'The love of my life. Will you marry me?'

I said yes, of course, then immediately changed my clothes and fixed my hair before FaceTiming my parents and sister to tell them the good news. I like to think I'm not a purely superficial person, but there are some moments that you know will be immortalised in screengrabs and selfies and you simply don't want to be wearing lemon yellow sweatpants for eternity.

Two weeks later, I was pregnant.

A few months previously, we had decided, if not to start *trying* to have a baby, then at least to stop trying *not* to. I had told Brandin all about the fertility testing I had undergone, and how I had been told that my woeful lack of eggs would make falling pregnant a challenge. Frankly, I didn't think I would be able to get pregnant – and so eschewing any preventative measures seemed like a mere formality.

As it happens, you really do just need one good egg, and mine was fertilised two weeks after he put a ring on it. America being America, this meant that we had to get married sooner rather than later, so that the baby and I could go on Brandin's health insurance plan, an option available only for one's spouse.

We had a town hall ceremony that March, attended by my sister, my eldest nephew, two of Brandin's friends and his mum. I'd bought a new dress for the occasion – navy, with coloured hearts all over it – and my sister gave me a small bouquet of flowers she'd bought in the bougie supermarket near her house on the way. Afterwards, we went for cocktails on the patio of a bar across the road, and drank them with tortilla chips and queso.

Brandin's friends had brought us a small cake; we sliced it under the heaters as the evening cooled, and toasted to the long, happy lives we hoped we'd have with our soon-to-be-three children.

I wasn't expecting marriage to change much between us, but I had underestimated the power of that little piece of paper. Now, when I find myself beginning to wonder whether or not Brandin *truly* loves me, or if he thinks about me during the day, as I think about him, I realise that it doesn't matter. We're married now. We own a couch together, a dog, Vinny, and a cat, Mel Brooks, we adopted from the shelter.

We even have a baby now, Atlas, born in October 2021 under the watchful eyes of both Brandin and my sister. It would have to be an extreme transgression for me to walk away now and free him from the shackles of this insomniac infant.

When we argue, now, it is less about how he expresses himself – 'Telling me you love me isn't *enough*,' I told him once, as he gazed at me in a state of absolute confusion, 'I need to *feel* it' – and more about why he didn't wash up his pan after breakfast; how I somehow manage to do laundry while watching the baby; which of us agreed to pick the boys up from school, or to sit through another two-hour soccer practice.

It is mundane but it is comforting, too. *He can't get away*, I think to myself sometimes. *It would be altogether too messy, and I doubt he wants the expense of another divorce.*

Epilogue

Sometimes I miss dating. When I catch a glimpse of myself in the bathroom mirror and I see my thirty-eight-year-old body and the ruination wrought upon it by my baby, I think I'd quite like to go on a date where some stranger could tell me I'm sexy.

I occasionally crave the validation you can only get from the kind of empty passion that comes from a one-night stand. I'd like to know that someone had swiped right on a photograph of my face and thought, *Yeah, I'd give her a go.*

Writing this book has, in a lot of ways, been a great cure for that kind of unhinged yearning. As I trawled through the archives of my dating past and relived each and every awkward, awful, uncomfortable moment, I did not find myself thinking wistfully about those times in my life. Instead, I found myself thinking sympathetically about the person I was in those times in my life.

If you've got this far, you'll know just how much of my time – precious time, I realise this now – I spent bending to the will of others, or, at the very least, to my perception of that will. I've spent far too many hours wondering what this man would like me to wear; how this man would prefer me to act. And for what?

In a sense, it's all been in pursuit of what I have now: a husband. A baby. A family. A love that can only be withdrawn through legal channels. A house in both of our names. The sense of security that comes with all of the aforementioned. A ring. (Two rings.)

It would be churlish of me to suggest that it wasn't worth it, the work I had to put in to get here. Because the end result – the outcome – is wonderful, right? I have a husband I love and who loves me. I have a baby who seems like the most miraculous miracle of miracles, even if he is a poor conversationalist and has terrible table manners. I have two stepsons who are funny and dramatic and ridiculous and unpredictable and exhausting and adorable. I wouldn't give any of them back. But I do wonder if it could have been achieved in a different way.

If I could turn back time, I would tell myself to worry a little bit less about being polite and spend a bit more time being firm. I would reassure myself: it's okay to change your mind.

I would sit myself down and give myself a long, persuasive talk about how asking someone to be honest with you is not *being demanding*; expecting respect and consideration is not *being desperate*; suggesting that a prospective romantic partner put some thought and effort into their date ideas is not *asking for too much*. It's not even asking for a lot. It is, in fact, asking for the bare minimum.

I would explain to myself that, while being loved – and loving someone, in turn – feels *great*, there are other things that feel great, too, like taking a holiday on your own (I went to the south of France for two weeks in my twenties and have never enjoyed myself as much as I did then, getting up when I felt like it, lying on the beach for as long as I liked, eating in whatever restaurant took my fancy, with zero compromise required); masturbating in the shower; ordering a two-course takeout meal and having half of it left to eat the following day; *not* having to share your Terry's Chocolate Orange with anyone else; watching whatever terrible dating reality shows you want without a dissenting voice in the room; sliding in between cold sheets on a hot night, entirely alone.

In some cultures, they believe that the very act of being photographed costs you something – that with every rendering of your image, a part of your soul is taken, forever affixed to that photograph. Each snapshot of my dating life feels a bit like that, as if a part of me was taken by that experience, suspended in amber, stuck in that moment, with that person, to grapple with that decision forever more.

There is no point in feeling sorry for the things I did, the people I gave myself to, the parts of myself I gave away – I can't change any of it.

But I can forgive myself.

A lot of the things that I have done ended up hurting someone. Very occasionally, I hurt someone else – but mostly, I hurt myself. I made myself small. I berated myself for not being strong enough, or hot enough, or 'cool' enough for some insignificant man who did not deserve my time or my effort.

I opened up my chest and I laid my heart bare and I allowed it to be chipped away at. I am sorry for that. (And I am forgiven, too.)

I hope that, the more we can talk about these experiences – about the moments we should have been more ourselves, instead of less; when we should have spoken up, instead of piping down – the less likely they are to repeat in future generations.

I look at young women on social media today, sharing their opinions and making jokes and baring their bellies and their hearts and I think, *good for you*. Be more, not less.

To all the boys I've loved before: I forgive you too. But really, it was never about you.

Acknowledgements

There are too many people to thank – said every acknowledgements section ever – and before I even try, I would like to say thank you to the hundreds, maybe even thousands, of people who have subscribed to my work, read my articles, commented on my social media posts, sent messages and (especially) those who have sat down to email me, whatever the topic. Without the support of these passionate, engaged, sometimes argumentative and always thought-inspiring women, I would never have had the confidence to sit down and commit these memories to the page. You have given me something invaluable, and I will never be able to thank you enough for it.

To all the team at Unbound, for supporting me through a long, sometimes arduous process of writing and rewriting (and rewriting again), but in particular to Katy Guest, for taking my memories under her wing, and to DeAndra Lupu, for having the patience of a thousand saints. And to Mark Ecob and Ben Tallon, whose design talents made the cover art as striking and memorable as I'd hoped.

Thank you to the girls, both of the parish and *not* of the parish: Róisín, Clare, Ciara, Emma, Ellen, Kate, Eimear, Aoife and anyone else I'm forgetting. Thank you for being with me through all of my mistakes and missteps, and never judging me for either.

A thanks, too, to my new girl crew, on the other side of the Atlantic: Hannah, Kailey, Katie, Bethany, Kerry and Kim. Thank you for being open to this new friendship of ours (and for always being on hand with a coffee).

To Brenda Mhic Ginneá, for being the kind of school principal I feared and loved in equal measure. Thank you for trying to teach me not to take myself too seriously, and for being hilarious and kind and loving and supportive, long after it had stopped being your job to do so.

Thank you to all of the friends who have, whether they like it or not, become my unofficial work wives: Kirstie McDermott, Aoibhinn Mc Bride, Sophie White and Lisa Bradley (who can always be counted on to have the most intelligent, well-reasoned take). Rose-anne Smith, for always believing in me, and taking on honorary godmother duties; and Caren Cregan, for staying up late when no one else does, and sending the best surprises in the post.

To Liam, you are an amazing support, advisor and critic, and the closest thing to a soulmate I could ever imagine (especially as I don't believe in soulmates).

To Beatrice, my best friend, whose advice I rarely ask for and almost never take, for being the best sister and aunt; the best editor and sounding board and ideas generator; the best shopping buddy and work buddy and exercise buddy, who always makes extra lasagne so I have some for my freezer and who never gets angry when I cancel our plans.

To Brandin, who's already told me he won't be reading this book, so will never see this: you are the tallest man I know. Congratulations. (I love you.)

To my mum and dad, for always reading my work, even when they don't approve of the subject matter; for reminding me, over and over again, that I curse too much; for showing me what kind of parent I'd like to be (and reminding me to check the best before dates on my cupboard staples). I love you so much, and I am so lucky to be your daughter.

And finally, to Atlas, Finn, William, Fox, Chance, Beau and Nash, the best boys I know. You've taught me patience (so much patience!) and forgiveness, and you've brought so much joy and fun and laughter into my life. The world is better because you're all in it, and you give me so much hope for this next generation of men. If they're anything like you, the future is going to be a far better place.

A Note on the Author

Rosemary Mac Cabe is a journalist and writer from Dublin, Ireland. She has written for publications including the *Irish Times*, *Irish Independent*, *Irish Tatler*, *IMAGE*, *Irish Country Magazine*, *STELLAR* and more. Her work was featured in the mental health anthology *You, Me & Everyone We Know*, published by Inspire Ireland. *This Is Not About You* is her first book.

@RosemaryMacCabe

Unbound is the world's first crowdfunding publisher, established in 2011.

We believe that wonderful things can happen when you clear a path for people who share a passion. That's why we've built a platform that brings together readers and authors to crowdfund books they believe in – and give fresh ideas that don't fit the traditional mould the chance they deserve.

This book is in your hands because readers made it possible. Everyone who pledged their support is listed below. Join them by visiting unbound.com and supporting a book today.

Aoife Abbey
Sarah Acton
Ciara Allen
Ursula Allen
R. Ambrose
Gillian Anderson
Amy Ashe
Annie Atkins
Aoife Austin
Ros Ball
Eoin Bannon
Ciara Bardon
Aisling Barrett

Louise Barrett
Michelle Barrett
Vikki Bayman
Helen Beatty
Conor Behan
Dagmar Bennett
Rachel Bennett
Lisa Blake
Allison Bolger
Emily Bolton-Hale
Niamh Bonney
Eleanor Booth
Siobhain Boyce

Ailish Bradley
Aoife Bradley
Catherine Bradley
Kat Brady
Michelle Brady
Anouska Proetta
   Brandon
Andrea Branley
Mary Ellen Breen
Rachel Breen
Anna Marie Brennan
Jillian Brett
Suzanne Brett
Mary Brien
Maeve Britton
Mel Broderick
Kim Brown
Kat Buckley
Naomi Buckley
Caitriona Burke
Roisin Burke
Anita Burleigh
Sarah Burns
Caoimhe Butler
Jean Butler
Breda Byrne
Caroline Byrne
Cathy Byrne
Edel Byrne
Elaine Byrne
Pamela Byrne

Stephanie Byrnes
Grace C
Caitriona C T
Niamh Cacciato
Caroline Caffrey
Niamh Cahalan
Caroline Cahill
Lisa Cal
Carla Callaghan
Aoife Campbell
Gabrielle Campion
Kelly Canham
Paula Cannon
Aoife Carey
Jennifer Carroll
Laura Carroll
Marguerite Carroll
Michelle Carroll
Sinead Carty
Annie Casey
Elizabeth Casey
Jean Casey
Patricia Casey
Fiona Cashin
Leah Caul
Orla Caulfield
Linda Christie
Chuy
Briona Claffey
Kevina Cleary
Mary Clifford

Sinead Clifford
Maria Clinch
Caitrina Cody
Aoife Coffey
Fiona Coffey
Nadine Cole
Mary Coleman
Aoife Collery
Aishling Collins
Amy Collins
Bree Collins
Helen Collins
Mary Collins
Tracy Collins
Jennifer Comaskey
Aisling Condren
Iseult Conlan
Clare Conneally
Ciara Conneely
Oonagh Connolly
Mrs Michelle Connolly-
   Glynn
Fiona Conway
Linda Conway
Moira Conway
Ami Cook
Harry Cooke
Amy Copeland
Suzie Corbett
Leonie Corcoran
Susanne Corr

Kitty Corridor
Aoife Corrigan
Deirdre Corrigan
Ilona Costelloe
Cathriona Cotter
Catherine Cottney
Jennifer Coughlan
Darragh and Saoirse
   Coughlan O Connor
Elizabeth Coulter
Cliodhna Coyle
Hannah Crehan
Olga Criado
Ashling Cronin
Nessa Cronin
Una Cronin
Katie Crossan
Marie Crowley
Sarah Crowley
Sophie Crowther
Christine Cuddy
Sara Cuddy
Fíona Cuffe
Cathy Cullen
Emer Cullen
Laura Cullen
Louise Cully
Emily Cunnane
Hannah Cunningham
Sarah Cunningham
Christine Curley

Roisin Curran
Megan D'Arcy
Jane Davis
Sinéad Davis
Ella De Guzman
Cliona de Paor
Michaela Deane
Regina Deegan
Aislinn Dellott
Louise Dempsey
Sheena Dempsey
Elaine Denehan
Paula Dennan
Ruth Devlin
Saranne Devlin
Marianna Di Murro
Karen Diffley
Maria Diffley
Zoe Dillon
Rachel Dincoff
Sarah Dineen
Claudia Divilly
Amy Dolan
Aisling Dollard
Aoife Dolphin
Jean Dolphin
Breda Donlon
Kiara Donnelly
Róisín Donnelly
Sarah Donnelly
Suzy Donnelly

Lola Donoghue
Ava Dooley
Karina Dooley
Lauren Dooley
Richard Doran
Emma Dougan
Bridget Douglas
Jennifer Douglas
Louise Dowling
Aifric Downey
Gemma Downey
Aisling Doyle
Angela Doyle
Ellen Doyle
Jane Doyle
Keira Doyle
Louise Doyle
Nicola Doyle
Orlagh Doyle
Sarah Doyle
Emma Duane
Emer Duffy
Lorna Duffy
Róisín Duffy
Carolyn Duggan
Brid Dunne
Louise Dunne
Niamh Durkin
Jen Dwyer
Nadine Dwyer
Maebh Egan

Sarah Egan
Shireen Egan
Amanda Eglite
Katie Eileen
Elaine
Yvonne Ellard
Michele Emerson
Remy English
Lauren Estes
Bláthna Everett
Catherine F
Jennifer F
Aoife Fannin
Aoife Farrell
Bébhinn Farrell
Eleanor Farrell
Emma Farrell
Tracey Farrell
Kellie Faul
Yvonne Feehan
Niamh Feely
Fiona Fegan
Patric ffrench Devitt
Kate Finlay
Roisin Finnegan
Sinead Finnegan
Kerry Fisher
Josephine Fitzgerald
Katie Fitzgerald
Niamh Fitzgerald
Rachel Fitzgerald

Sharon Fitzgerald
Niamh Fitzpatrick
Siobhán Fitzpatrick
Sheila Flaherty
Aoife Fleming
Grainne Fleury
Allison Flynn
Clare Flynn
Ellen Flynn
Karen Flynn
Marian Flynn
Melissa Flynn
Rebecca Flynn
Treasa Flynn
Dolores Fogarty
Maryann Folan
Kiara Ford
Clare Fowler
Kristan Fox
Catherine Furey
Sära Furlong
Niamh Gaffney
Niamh Gaine
Amanda Gallagher
Naomh Galloway
Nicola Galvin
Grace Gannon
Simone Gannon
Abby Garcia
Jessica Gaughran
Louise Gaughran

Brenda Gavin
Lynn Genevieve
Martina Genockey
Liam Geraghty
Donna Gilligan
Deborah Gilmartin
Caoimhe Good
Gemma Gorevan
Caoimhe Gorman
Gemma Gorman
Claire Gormley
Katharine Gosling
Sophie Grace
Grace
Aoife Graham
Audrey Graham
Lucy Graham
Michelle Graham
Jennifer Greaves
Una Greene
Aisling Griffin
Rebecca Griffin
Lorna Griffith
Nicola Gryson
Katy Guest
Eimear Guidera
Amy Guilfoyle
Natasha Gunnell
C H
Lavisa Hackett
Sophie Halpin

Gillian Hamill
Aisling Hamill-Fitzgerald
Aoife Hand
Anne Hanley
Katriona Hannon
Sorcha Hannon
Stephen Harding
Tracy Hardy
Fiona "Hargie"
    Hargadon
Colin Harmon
Katie Harrington
Peter Harrison
Kerri Hastings
Caroline Hayes
Maeve Healy
Heartland Society of
    Women Writers
Andie Hefferon
Emer Hehir
Claire Henderson
Emma Henderson
Laura Henderson
Debbie Hennebry
Claire Hennessy
Margaret-Anne
    Hennessy
Michelle Hennessy
Peggy Hennessy
Natasha Henry
Ruth Henshaw

Therese Herlihy
Kate Hession
Colette Hester
Ronan Hickey
Nuala Higgins
Rachel Hill
Marina Hogan
Melissa Holden
Jane Holian
Mairead Holohan
Aisling Hopkins
Aoife Horan
Emily Horgan
Niamh Howard
Rachel Howe
Marie-Ann Hughes
Róna Hunt
Barbara Hurley
Karina Hutchinson
Michali Hyams
Laura Hyde
Fiona Hynes
Carla Inglis
Yasmeen Islam
Julie Jay
Vanessa Job
Maria Johnston
Fionnuala Jones
Joanne Jordan
Jennifer Joyce
Kate Joyce

Pollyanna Joyce
Claire Kane
Gráinne Kavanagh
Sarah Kavanagh
Una Kavanagh
Digby KDB
Dee Keane
Elaine Keane
Lucy Keane
Aoife Kearns
Evelyn Kearns
Amy Keating
Yvonne Keating
Carly Keegan
Ciara Keegan
Patrice Keegan
Denise Kelleher
Aine Kelly
Alice Kelly
Archie Kelly
Caoimhe Kelly
Claire Kelly
Justice Kelly
Laura Kelly
Rachael Kelly
Sarah Kelly
Tracey Kelly
Avril Kennedy
Claire Kennedy
Maria Kennedy
Niamh Kennedy

Rachel Kennedy
Sarah-Anne Kennedy
Tracey Kennedy
Aoife Kenny
Fiona Kenny
Shanna Kenny
Edward Kenyi
Louise Keogh
Sinead Keohane
Cara Kerrigan
Dan Kieran
Claudia Kilpatrick
Lucy Kilroy
Shona King
Colette Kinsella
Emma Kinsella
Karina Kinsella
Miriam Kinsella
Lorraine Kirk
Karen Kirwan
Kate Kirwan
Sarah Kirwan
Cara Lally
Katie Lally
Ciara Landy
Emma Langford
Elaine Lavery
Marie Lavin
Ciara Lawler
Amanda Lee
Laura Lee

Niamh Leneghan
Karen Lennon
Leoina Lennon
Megan Lennon
Sharon Lennon
Katie Linden
Samantha Lloyd
Tracey Long
Rosie Loye
Caroline Lunney
Aoife Lynch
Caroline Lynch
Elisa Lynch
Gemma Lynch
Sooby Lynch
Deirdre Lyons
Kate Lyons
Maeve Lyons
B M
Beatrice Mac Cabe
Philip Mac Cabe
Sinéad Mac Namara
Maeve MacCabe
Niall and Mary
   MacCabe
Áine Madden
Christine Maguire
Eamonn Maguire
Sasha Maguire
Emily Maher
Michelle Mahon

Catt** Makin

Minna Makinen

Carol Ann Malone

Sinead Malone

Melodie Manners

Lisa Manselli

Sarah Manvel

Claire Manzor

Rachel Marsden

Emily Marshall

Naomi Martin

Nicola Martin

Ruth Martin

Bryan Martyn

Rebecca Mason

Aoibhinn Mc Bride

Aoife Mc Carthy

Donna Mc Connell

Nicola Mc Nally

Ciara Mc Nelis

Olivia McAleese

Nicola McArdle

Niamh McAteer

Rebecca McAteer

Niamh McCabe

Ursula McCabe

Sarah McCann

Eimear McCarthy

Rachel McCarthy

Anne McCarvill

Ríoghnach McCaughey

Beth McColl

Paula Mccool

Hilda McCormack

Sarah McCormack

Megan McCormick

Kirstie Mcdermott

Susan McDermott

Sarah Mcdonagh

Jeanie McDonald

Richéal McDonald

Sarah Mcdonald

Tara McElligott

Sharon McEneaney

Paula McEntee

Grainne McFeely

Grace McGeever

Aoife McGlone

Gemma McGrane

Fiona McGrath

Kate McGrath

Lisa Mcgrath

Martina McGrath

Amy McGuinness

Lorraine McHugh

Ciara McInerney

Eve McInerney

Kathy McIntyre

Edel McKendry

Julie McKenna

Caroline McKeown

Marianne McKnight

Jane McLaughlin
Maeve McLaughlin
Roisin McLaughlin
Danielle McMahon
Eimear McMahon
Aoife McMenamin
Jenny McNamara
Claire McNeela
Katie McRory
Tara McS
Mairead McTigue
Chloe Meehan
Marian Meehan
Sarah-Rose Meehan
Aoife Merrigan
Louise Merrigan
John Mitchinson
Molly Moclair
Anne Marie Moloney
Linda Monckton
Lyndsay Montina
Alison Moore
Bernadette Moore
Claire Moore
Sarah Moraghan
Lynn Morgan
Paula Morgan
Janette Moriarty
Kate Moriarty
Lorraine Morrin
Jennifer Mortell

Vicki Mountjoy
Dee Mulcahy
Lesley Mulhall
Claire Mulholland
Lorraine Mulkerrins
Lizzy Mulligan
Rosemarie Mullin
Darragh Mullooly
Karen Mulreid
Katy Mulvenna
Lauren Mulville
Aoife Murphy
Cara Murphy
Caroline Murphy
Ciara Murphy
Clare Murphy
Elaine Murphy
Emma Murphy
Joanne Murphy
Louise Murphy
Lucy Murphy
Maria Murphy
Michelle Murphy
Nicola Murphy
Sinead Murphy
Caitríona Murphy
    O'Reilly
Róisín Murray
Sarah Murray
Louise Murtagh
Michelle Nagle

Sarah-Louise Nandadasa
Fiona Nash
Shauna Nash
Carlo Navato
Linda Nee
Nat Nestor
Jennifer Newman
Kirby Newton
Ruth Ní Bheoláin
Caoilfhionn Ni
  Chuanachain
Laura Ni Mhorda
Deirdre Ní Shúilleabháin
Siobhán NicÓda
Meaghan Nolan
Maria Noonan
Niamh Noonan
Siobhan Noonan
Natalie Noone
Ciara Norton
Jean Norton
Vanessa Nowak
Lesley Nugent
Eimear O Callaghan
Denise O Connell
Laura O Connell
Craig O Connor
Laura O Connor
Orla O Connor
Niamh O Donnell
Heather O Donoghue

Niamh O Neill
Aine O Reilly
Darinagh Doran O Reilly
Lisa-Jane O Riordan
Siobhan O Rourke
Aoibhinn O Sullivan
Clíona O Sullivan
Marie O Sullivan
Ailis O'Brien
Joanne O'Brien
Roisin O'Brien
Sarah O'Brien
Sinead O'Brien
Eimear O'Carroll
Aisling O'Connor
Deirdre O'Connor
Teresa O'Connor
Zoe O'Connor
Laura O'Dea
Roisín O'Doherty
Sarah O'Donovan
Claire O'Dowd
Lisa O'Farrell
Noreen O'Gorman
Nessa O'Hara
Shauna O'Hara
Charlotte O'Kane
Maeve O'Malley
Danielle O'Meara
Caoimhe O'Neill
Dervla O'Neill

Emma O'Neill
Grace O'Reilly
Jenny O'Reilly
Niamh O'Reilly
B O'Riordan
Lauren O'Rourke
Aisling O'Sullivan
Janice O'Sullivan
Katie O'Sullivan
Killian O'Sullivan
Siobhán O'Sullivan
Aliosn O'Brien
Mary O'Brien
Caoimhe O'Connor
Debbie O'Connor
Maeve O'Connor
Lily O'Donnell
Marguerite O'Donovan
Dairín O'Driscoll
Vicky O'Gorman
Niamh O'Grady
Joanne O'Halloran
Nicolle O'Keeffe
Ciara O'Neill
Louise O'Neill
Holly O'Riordan
Caroline O'Shea
Aisling O'Sullivan
Aoife O'Sullivan
Fiona O'Sullivan
Taryn OHara

Jean Oneill
Orla
Rachel Oswell
Caroline Owens
Emma Ozenbrook
Lorraine Paisley
AnneMarie Peake
Julie Peelo
Helen Perry
PG
Emma Phelan
Ruth Phelan
Sarah Jane Phelan
Suzanne Phelan
Justin Pollard
Alan Powell
Catherine Powell
Dawn Prendergast
Linda Prendergast
Meghan Price
Dee Purcell
Siobhan Purcell
Tess Purcell
Tricia Purcell
Emma Purser
Caroline Quane
Aoife Quinn
Nichole Quinn
Leah Quirke
Cathy Rabinovich
Orlaith Rafferty

Kim Raggett

Maureen Reavey

Denise Redding Korte

Miriam Reidy

Joanne Reilly

Roisin Reilly

Hannah Rice

Louise Robinson-Daley

Kelley Rogers

Marie Rohan

Aimee Rondthaler

Danika Rooney

Laura Rooney

Rachel Rooney

Leanne Ross

Ciara Ruane

Aileen Ryan

Aine Ryan

Brid Ryan

Finn Ryan

Lisa Ryan

Lorraine Ryan

Rosemary Ryan

Sinead Ryan

Jenny Rynne

Genny Salman

Evie Sammon

Isobel Sarsfield

J. Scanlan

Jennie Scanlan

Hannah Schmitz

Johanna Seeber

Aileen Shah

Mary Shanahan

Laurence Shapiro

Anne Sharkey

Sian Sharkey

Mairead Sheehan

Gillian Sheehy

Emma Sheridan

Kacey Sheridan

Emma Shiel

Louise Shorten

Síle

Pamela Skaufel

Aine Slater

Hazel Slavin

Andrea Smith

Anna Smith

Deirdre Smith

Elizabeth Smith

Lilian Smith

Roseanne Smith

Susan Smith

Sarah Smyth

Sharon Somers

Ruth Somerville

Emer Spain

Niamh Staveley

Jennifer Stevens

Ruth Stevens

Philip Stewart

Dee StJohn
Lorraine StJohn
Kailey Stockburger
Aoife Stones
Sinéad Strnadel
Aisling O Sullivan
L. Sullivan
A Supporter
Jean Sutton
Cora Sutton-Smith
Elaine Sweeney
Seana Sweeney
Tracy Sweeney
Fiona Swords
Minte Taekema
Clara Talbot
Emer Thompson
Yvonne Tiernan
Emma Timoney
Donna Toher
Marie Tormey
Natasha Touhey
Louise Tracey
Helen Trainor
Fiona Treacy
Sarah Troy
Daniella Morrison
   Twamley
Fíona Uí Mhainnín
Katia Valadeau
Clodagh Vance

Aisling Vaughan
Megan Vaughan
Sorcha Versteeg
Jose Miguel Vicente
   Luna
Aisling Wadding
Aisling Wall
Emer Wall
Jenny Wall
Brandin Wallace
Kelly Wallace
Trina Wallace
Virginia Wallace
Aisling Walsh
Eimear Walsh
Eleanor Walsh
Holly Walsh
Jayann Walsh
Marie Walsh
Moira Walsh
Jennie Walshe
Jennifer Ward
Helena Whelan
Sheila Whelan
Aisling White
Chelsea White
Michelle White
Sophie White
Faye Whitfield
Whitney
Rosetta Whyte

Supporters

Rebecca Wickens
Mary Willis
Deirdre Wilson
Sasha Wilson
Wimp Wimp
Catherine Woods

Danielle Woods
Lisa Woods
Ruth Woods
Tara Wynne
Sheena Wyse
Matt Zitron